the ADRIATIC Kitchen

About the author

Barbara Unković was born in New Zealand, the daughter of a Croatian father and an English mother. She is D.H. Lawrence's cousin. Barbara holds a Master of Creative Writing from the University of Auckland in New Zealand and is the recipient of more than 30 writing awards from the United Kingdom and the United States of America. Her published titles include: *Adriatic Blue*, *Weeds in the Garden of Eden*, *A Wolf in Sheep's Clothing*, *Moon Walking*, *Furry Blur* and *Naughty Noosa Meets the New Neighbours*.

For more detailed information about Barbara, please visit her website at www.barbaraunkovic.com.

the
ADRIATIC
Kitchen

Recipes inspired by the abundance
of seasonal ingredients flourishing on
the Croatian island of Korčula

BARBARA UNKOVIĆ

EXISLE
PUBLISHING

First published 2017

Exisle Publishing Pty Ltd
'Moonrising', Narone Creek Road, Wollombi, NSW 2325, Australia
P.O. Box 60–490, Titirangi, Auckland 0642, New Zealand
www.exislepublishing.com

A CiP record for this book is available from the National Library of Australia.

ISBN 978-1-925335-36-1

Designed by Big Cat Design
Typeset in Adobe Caslon Pro 10 on 16pt
Printed in China

This book uses paper sourced under ISO 14001 guidelines from well-managed
forests and other controlled sources.

2 4 6 8 10 9 7 5 3 1

Dedication

This book is dedicated to my husband Denis, whom I would like to thank for his continued support, encouragement and tireless tending of our organic gardens and olive trees.

Denis was a well-known chef and coffee roaster in the vibrant café and restaurant scene in Wellington, New Zealand, during the eighties and nineties. He owned a number of popular establishments including The Paté Shop, Turnbull House, Bowen Street Café and The Begonia Café.

In 1999, we set up Café 51 in Wellington, followed by Costa Noosa Espresso in Queensland's Noosa Heads, Australia, in 2003. By this time, Denis had moved on to become a highly skilled coffee roaster, while I took over supervision of the kitchen and menu design together with my duties as a chef. Although working together proved to be tough at times, we made a great team and I always admired Denis' passion, drive and dedication.

A special thank you also to my daughter Rebecca Fletcher for her invaluable assistance, and to my brother Colin Unkovich for creating the sensational artwork.

Contents

Autumn

Winter

Introduction

On my first visit to the island of Korčula I was both astonished and delighted by the abundance of edible seasonal delights flourishing around me. This, combined with the natural beauty of the island, was largely responsible for me choosing to make the island my home.

As I watched the days turn into months and the months evolve into seasons, in the village of Račišće, it seemed only natural to put together this recipe book.

Croatian cuisine is particularly regional and the specialties differ greatly from the mountainous regions of the interior, to the Dalmatian Coast with its hundreds of islands. In Slavonia, in the north-east of Croatia, you will encounter kulen, a hot spicy salami; whereas if you visit Korčula, you will discover pršut, a dried smoked ham, and the renowned black risotto. During my time here I have been fortunate to taste many traditional Croatian foods and dishes.

The influences in Croatian cuisine are varied and come from Italy, Turkey and Austria.

Croatian people have lived off the fruit of the land and the sea for several thousands of years. They harvest and enjoy wild fruit, home-grown vegetables and wild herbs including sage and oregano. Asparagus, capers, mushrooms, olives, figs, pomegranates and blackberries also flourish freely here. The Adriatic Sea, which surrounds the island of Korčula, yields a boundless variety of seafood including anchovies, squid, octopus, mackerel and eel.

Throughout Croatia, the main meal of the day is often a drawn-out affair commonly eaten in the middle of the day. The meal does not begin without a glass of aperitif or rakija, the fiery homemade spirits brewed by the locals. There are many different varieties, and on this island the more common ones are walnut or herb, and the most unusual one, blueberry. This long lunch is invariably accompanied by excellent local wine. Here on Korčula we are privileged to enjoy Grk, a dry white from the village of Lumbarda; Plavac, a rich, fragrant red from Blato, Žrnovo, and Pupnat;

and Rukatac, an aromatic white from Čara and Smokvića. The combination of excellent wine and superb food ensures a marvellously tasty meal.

This book is not intended to feature only Croatian recipes, but recipes inspired by the fantastic range of fresh, seasonal produce available in this small sleepy village with its lush vegetation, rich fertile soil and hot, endless summers.

My recipes have been tried and tested many times and I pride myself on using only the finest, freshest, seasonal ingredients, extra virgin olive oil, sea salt and freshly ground black or distinctive green pepper.

It is my desire to share with you my passion for simple, creative cuisine inspired by the bountiful fresh fare of the beautiful Adriatic.

Spring

This is one of my favourite times of the year. On the Dalmatian Coast spring is usually short and sharp, stretching from March until May. As soon as winter departs the temperature often increases from 13°C (55°F) to 23°C (73°F) in the space of merely a few days. Spring arrives almost overnight and even though I know this is the case, I cannot seem to get used to it. At this time of year, the landscape is a profusion of beautiful flowers. One of the most spectacular sights is the pink and white blossoms on the numerous almond trees. They begin flowering in January. By March, when they reach their blooming peak, the trees are smothered with delicate, snow-like flowers. Fields are dotted with daffodils, wild snapdragons, bright red poppies and vibrant, purple sage. Ancient stone walls are covered with small wild flowers, white daisies and the tiniest bright pink, delicate cyclamen. The countless olive trees are smothered with small, white star-like flowers and in May, tiny vivid tangerine blossoms open on pomegranate stems against a backdrop of small yet bright green, glossy leaves. Hillsides no longer cultivated or maintained are ablaze with bright yellow broom. Spring is the time for preparing this rich fertile soil before planting a multitude of seeds and seedlings. At the end of winter, the landscape is at last awake and alive. It is a joy to behold the beauty of spring in this lush, green land.

Peasant Bread

Zvon, a young enthusiastic Croatian chef from Zagreb, shared this recipe with me. It was traditionally baked under a metal or earthenware *peka* or bell covered with burning embers from a hot, open fire. Today, it can be baked successfully in a very hot fan-forced oven. To produce a boost of steam to help ensure a strong, even crust, pour a cup of water into a dish in the bottom of the oven immediately before you close the door to begin baking the loaf.

Ingredients:

250 grams (about 2 cups) strong bread flour (high gluten content)

250 grams (about 2 cups) plain flour

2 teaspoons salt

2 tablespoons olive oil

8 grams (1 tablespoon) fresh yeast, crumbled

2 teaspoons sugar

1 tablespoon liquid honey

500 millilitres (2 cups) tepid water, approximate

- In a large bowl, sift together the two types of flour. Using a knife, make two indentations in the flour — one on each side. In the first indentation add the salt followed by the oil. In the second indentation, rub in the yeast using your fingertips. Add the sugar and honey to this indentation.

- Add water to the yeast, honey combination. Mix, pulling in the surrounding flour.

- Next, add water to the salt, oil combination and mix into the surrounding flour. Combine the two sections of flour, beginning with the yeast area first, and mix all the ingredients together with sufficient water to form a soft dough.

- Turn the dough out onto a lightly floured board (if you can knead without flour, so much the better). Knead for 10 minutes until it is smooth and elastic.

- Shape the dough into a ball and coat the top with olive oil. Place in an oiled stainless steel bowl and cover with a baking cloth or clean tea towel. Leave it to rise for 30 minutes in a warm place.

- Flatten the dough, reshape into a ball and leave it to rise again for 30 minutes. Repeat.

- When shaping the dough into a ball for a third and final rise, ensure there is a spine or seam on the underside of the dough. This helps the loaf retain its shape during baking.

- Place the dough on a lightly floured baking tray. Leave uncovered and let rise once more for 30 minutes.

- Preheat the oven to 200°C (400°F).

- At the end of last rise, oil the top of the dough thoroughly.

- Bake for 20–25 minutes. The loaf should sound hollow when tapped. Remove from the oven, wrap in a clean tea towel and cool on a wire rack.

Croatian Sweet Easter Bread

KNOWN IN CROATIA AS *SIRNICA*, THIS EASTER TREAT IS SIMILAR TO THE
TRADITIONAL ITALIAN SWEET BREAD, *PANETTONE*. THE ADDITION OF CITRUS
ZEST, CRYSTALLIZED PEEL AND ALLSPICE MAKES THIS BREAD A SPECIAL
INDULGENCE.

Ingredients:

1 teaspoon sugar

60 millilitres (¼ cup) warm water

8 grams (1 tablespoon) fresh yeast, crumbled

185 millilitres (¾ cup) milk

75 grams (5 tablespoons) butter

500 grams (about 4 cups) plain flour, sifted

100 grams (about ½ cup) sugar

½ teaspoon salt

4 egg yolks, lightly beaten

¼ cup crystallized lemon peel (see recipe on page 31)

zest from 2 lemons

zest from 1 orange

1 teaspoon ground allspice

1 teaspoon freshly grated nutmeg

milk to brush

limoncello to glaze (see recipe on page 102)

vanilla sugar

- In a small bowl, dissolve the teaspoon of sugar in the warm water. Sprinkle yeast over the water. Set aside in a warm place for 10 minutes until frothy.

- Place milk and butter in a small saucepan. Stir over low heat until butter melts. Transfer to a large bowl and allow to cool until lukewarm. Stir in the frothy yeast mixture.

- Using a wooden spoon, beat in 125 grams (about 1 cup) of sifted flour, followed by the sugar and salt. Cover with plastic food wrap and leave in a warm place until bubbly (about 20–25 minutes).

- Mix the beaten egg yolks and the remaining sifted flour into the yeast mixture. Add the crystallized peel, lemon and orange zest, allspice and nutmeg. Mix to a soft dough using a knife. The dough must be very soft and almost difficult to handle. It may not be necessary to use all the flour.

- Turn the dough out onto a lightly floured board. Knead for 10 minutes until it is smooth and elastic.

- Shape the dough into a ball and coat with olive oil. Place in an oiled bowl and cover with a baking cloth or clean tea towel. Leave to rise in a warm place for 70–90 minutes, until almost doubled in size.

- Flatten the dough and knead for 1 minute on a lightly floured work surface. Shape into a ball, with the spine or seam on the underside. Cover with olive oil and place in a deep, oiled, 20 centimetre (8 inch) round cake tin. If the tin is too shallow, line the sides with baking paper extending it at least 12 centimetres (4–5 inches) above the rim of the tin.

- Score the top of the dough with 3 long deep cuts intersecting at the centre. The cuts need to be quite deep (at least halfway through the loaf) to allow the dough to rise up from the centre to form the traditional crests of Sirnica. Make the cuts swiftly and cleanly. Do not drag or pull the dough.

- Leave to rise in a warm place for 45 minutes.

- Preheat the oven to 190°C (375°F).

- Brush the top of the dough with milk.

- Bake for 10 minutes. Reduce oven temperature to 170°C (340°F) and bake for 20–30 more minutes until bread sounds hollow when tapped and a metal skewer comes out clean when inserted into the middle.

- Remove from the oven. Brush the top of the loaf generously with limoncello and sprinkle with vanilla sugar while hot. Leave in the tin for 10 minutes before transferring to a cooling rack.

- Serve at room temperature.

Focaccia Bread with Rocket (Arugula) and Cheese Filling

UNTIL THE END OF WWII, ISTRIA, IN THE NORTH OF CROATIA, WAS
ITALIAN TERRITORY. TODAY MANY OF THE INFLUENCES FROM ITALY CAN
STILL BE FOUND THERE AND THIS RECIPE IS ONE OF THEM.

Ingredients:

400 grams (about 3 cups) plain flour

8 grams (1 tablespoon) fresh yeast, crumbled

1 tablespoon olive oil, plus extra

2 teaspoons salt

tepid water to mix (see cooking notes on page 108)

80 grams (¾ cup) parmesan or aged cheddar, grated

large handful of rocket (arugula) leaves

2 tablespoons thyme, finely chopped

- Sift the flour into a large bowl. Rub in the yeast using your fingertips. Add olive oil and salt.
- Add sufficient water and mix to a firm dough.
- Turn the dough out onto a lightly floured board. Knead for 10 minutes until it is smooth and elastic.
- Shape the dough into a ball and place in a lightly floured bowl. Cover with a baking cloth or clean tea towel and leave to rise in a warm place for 1 hour.
- Remove the dough from the bowl and roll into a large rectangle. Drizzle one half with olive oil and sprinkle with the grated cheese and rocket (arugula). Drizzle again with olive oil.
- Fold over half the dough to cover the cheese and rocket (arugula). Seal the edges by pinching with your thumb and first finger. Rub a small quantity of oil on top of the bread and sprinkle with chopped thyme. Place on a lightly floured baking tray and leave in a warm place to rise for 1 hour.
- Preheat the oven to 200°C (400°F).
- Bake for 18–20 minutes until light golden brown. Cool on a wire rack.
- Serve drizzled with extra olive oil.

Focaccia Bread with Parmesan Cheese and Thyme

THIS RECIPE WAS ONE OF THE FIRST LOAVES I BEGAN TO BAKE IN RAČIŠĆE.
IN THE EARLY DAYS OF OUR LIFE HERE, THE BREAD IN THE VILLAGE
STORE TASTED MORE LIKE CARDBOARD AND WENT STALE TOO QUICKLY.
I REMEMBER WELL MY FIRST FOCACCIA LOAF. WE ENJOYED IT ON OUR
TERRACE IN THE BRIGHT SPRING SUNSHINE WITH A GLASS OF LOCAL, DRY
WHITE WINE.

Ingredients:

375 grams (about 3 cups) plain flour

8 grams (1 tablespoon) fresh yeast, crumbled

1 tablespoon olive oil, plus extra

2 teaspoons salt

tepid water to mix (see cooking notes on page 108)

2 tablespoons parmesan cheese, grated

2 tablespoons thyme, finely chopped

- Sift flour into a large bowl. Using your fingertips, rub in the yeast. Add olive oil and salt.
- Add sufficient water and mix to a firm dough.
- Turn the dough out onto a lightly floured board. Knead the dough for 10 minutes until it is smooth and elastic.
- Shape the dough into a ball and place in a lightly floured bowl. Cover with a baking cloth or clean tea towel and leave to rise in a warm place for 1 hour.
- Remove dough from the bowl and roll out into a circle 4 centimetres (1½ inches) thick. Place on a lightly floured baking tray.
- Using your fingers, push deep dents into the surface of the dough.
- Sprinkle with thyme and parmesan cheese, and drizzle generously with olive oil.
- Leave to rise in a warm place for 45 minutes.
- Preheat oven to 180°C (350°F).
- Bake for 20 minutes until pale golden brown. Cool on a wire rack.
- Serve drizzled with extra olive oil.

Roast Garlic

EVERY YEAR, IN MID DECEMBER, AROUND THE SHORTEST DAY OF THE YEAR, WE PLANT GARLIC. IT IS HARVESTED ON, OR JUST BEFORE, THE LONGEST DAY OF THE YEAR IN MID JUNE. MOST YEARS WE ENJOY A SUCCESSFUL CROP AND THE FOLLOWING RECIPE IS ONE OF MY FAVOURITES. WHEN THE TIME COMES TO HARVEST I ALWAYS HOPE FOR AN ABUNDANT CROP, SUFFICIENT TO PLAIT IT AND HANG IT IN MY KITCHEN AS IS THE CUSTOM HERE.

Ingredients:

4–6 heads garlic

olive oil

- Preheat the oven to 190°C (375°F) before preparing the garlic.
- Peel a few of the outer layers from each of the garlic heads, leaving the garlic cloves intact. Cut 1–2 centimetres (about ½ inch) from the top of the heads to barely expose the individual cloves.
- Place in a roasting pan lined with baking paper. Drizzle with the olive oil.
- Roast for 30 minutes until the garlic cloves are soft.

Carrot and Mint Salad

CARROTS ARE WELL SUITED TO THE CLIMATE HERE. THIS RECIPE WAS
SHARED WITH ME OVER TWENTY YEARS AGO BY MY FRIEND ROGER.
IT IS A RECIPE THAT ALWAYS ATTRACTS COMPLIMENTS. THIS EXCEPTIONAL
SALAD IS PERFECT FOR ENTERTAINING AS IT CAN BE MADE A COUPLE
OF DAYS AHEAD.

Ingredients:

4 large carrots

1 small onion, finely sliced

4 tablespoons fresh mint, finely
   chopped

250 millilitres (1 cup) homemade
   tomato purée

125 millilitres (½ cup) olive oil

185 millilitres (¾ cup) red wine vinegar

200 grams (about 1 cup) sugar

1 teaspoon wholegrain mustard

1 teaspoon Worcestershire sauce

- Peel the carrots, and slice into 2 centimetre (¾ inch) thick rounds. Cook for 20 minutes in boiling, salted water until tender. Drain, place in a bowl or on a platter and set aside to cool.

- Add the onion and mint.

- In a small saucepan, combine tomato purée, olive oil, vinegar, sugar, mustard and Worcestershire sauce. Bring to the boil, then reduce the heat and simmer for 4 minutes.

- Remove from the heat and pour over the carrots.

- Cover and refrigerate for 24 hours before serving.

Octopus Salad

I WAS FIRST INTRODUCED TO *SALATA OD HOBOTNICE* BY RANKO, THE STONEMASON RESTORING OUR HOUSE. EVERY MORNING, BEFORE HE STARTS HIS WORK DAY, YOU WILL FIND HIM WALKING ALONG THE WATER'S EDGE HOPING TO SPOT AN OCTOPUS IN THE CRYSTAL CLEAR WATER. THE JAG (BARBED HOOK) HE ALWAYS CARRIES IN HIS POCKET OFTEN COMES IN HANDY.

HIS ADVICE ON HOW TO CREATE THIS DISH INCLUDED A DEFINITE INSTRUCTION TO CLEAN THE FRESHLY CAUGHT OCTOPUS IN SALT WATER AND FREEZE IT FOR AT LEAST THREE DAYS BEFORE USING IT IN THIS SALAD. YOU CAN CLEAN AND PREPARE THE OCTOPUS YOURSELF OR ASK YOUR LOCAL FISHMONGER TO DO IT FOR YOU.

Ingredients:

1 kilogram (2¼ pounds) octopus

2 bay leaves

juice from 1 lemon

2 tablespoons parsley, finely chopped

2 tablespoons red wine vinegar

12 cherry tomatoes

2 tablespoons capers

2 garlic cloves, finely sliced

2 tablespoons olive oil

2 medium potatoes, cooked and diced

sea salt and black pepper

- Place the washed, cleaned octopus in a large pan and cover with water. Add the bay leaves.
- Place over medium heat and simmer for 1½–2 hours until tender. To check if the octopus is cooked, pierce the neck with a fork. There should be little or no resistance. Drain well.
- When it is cool, cut the octopus into small pieces and place in a large bowl.
- Add the remaining ingredients, mix gently and season to taste with salt and pepper. Refrigerate. Serve cold.

Pan-Fried Anchovies

During spring and summer, the blue fish truck is a regular visitor to our village and the anchovies sold by the father and his son provide a simple, inexpensive meal.

Whenever I eat anchovies I am always reminded of our friend Pavo's method of making brine to preserve anchovies for eating during winter. Pavo never weighs out the salt for the brine. He prefers to use a swimming potato. Unable to imagine what he meant the first time he said this, I stood back and watched while he stirred a handful of salt into a bucket of water before dropping in a potato.

'It is not necessary to weigh the salt. You must watch the potato. If he swims then the brine is the right strength,' Pavo said. This is one of the most amusing tales I have heard in this village, but it appears to work.

Ingredients:

30 grams (about ¼ cup) wholemeal (whole-wheat) flour

sea salt, black pepper and/or any seasoning of your choice, for example, lemon pepper

500 grams (about 1 pound) fresh anchovies with heads and insides removed (washed and cleaned in sea water)

olive oil

wedges of lemon

- Place the seasoned flour into a large brown paper bag.
- Add the anchovies, about 3 at a time. Shake the bag to coat the fish thoroughly.
- Shallow fry over medium heat, turning once after 1–2 minutes until fish are light golden brown. Do not overcook as the fish may fall apart.
- Remove and drain on kitchen paper.
- Serve hot, with wedges of lemon.

Four Cheese Pizza with Sage and Capers

PIZZA CAN BE FOUND IN MANY OF THE RESTAURANTS THROUGHOUT CROATIA. THERE ARE MANY EXCELLENT LOCAL CHEESES. TRAPPIST CHEDDAR, AN AGED CHEESE FROM THE ISLAND OF PAG, IS ONE OF THE FINEST.

Ingredients:

THE DOUGH

300 grams (about 2½ cups) plain flour

8 grams (1 tablespoon) fresh yeast, crumbled

1 tablespoon olive oil

2 teaspoons salt

tepid water to mix (see cooking notes on page 108)

THE TOMATO SAUCE

1 tablespoon olive oil

1 small onion, finely chopped

1 large garlic clove, crushed

4–5 tomatoes, blanched to remove the skins

2 tablespoons fresh basil leaves

½ red capsicum (bell pepper), finely sliced

sea salt and black pepper

THE TOPPING

400 grams (14 ounces) emmenthal cheese, grated

300 grams (10½ ounces) cheddar or hard cheese, grated

150 grams (5¼ ounces) gorgonzola or blue cheese, grated

200 grams (7 ounces) mozzarella, thinly sliced

1 tablespoon capers

handful of small fresh sage leaves

- Sift flour into a large bowl. Using your fingertips, rub in the yeast. Add olive oil and salt.
- Add sufficient water and mix to a firm dough.
- Turn dough out onto a lightly floured board. Knead for 10 minutes until it is smooth and elastic.
- Shape the dough into a ball and place in a lightly floured bowl. Cover with a baking cloth or clean tea towel. Leave to rise in a warm place for 1 hour.
- Meanwhile, assemble the ingredients for the topping.
- To make the tomato sauce, sauté the onion in olive oil until it is transparent. Add garlic, tomatoes, basil and capsicum (bell pepper).
- Simmer for 15–20 minutes until sauce is thick. Mash the tomatoes with a wooden spoon if they do not break up during the cooking.
- Season to taste with salt and pepper. Cool and set aside.
- Preheat the oven to 200°C (400°F). Place a pizza stone into the oven if you have one. This is not essential. You can substitute a heavy baking tray.
- Turn the dough onto a lightly floured work surface and roll out to fit the pizza stone or baking tray.
- Spread tomato sauce over the dough and scatter with the cheeses. Top with sage leaves and capers.
- Transfer the prepared pizza to the heated pizza stone or baking tray.
- Bake for 15–20 minutes until golden brown.
- Drizzle with olive oil and serve immediately.

Zucchini (Courgette) Fritters with Fresh Sage

SAGE IS WITHOUT A DOUBT ONE OF THE MOST ABUNDANT WILD HERBS GROWING HERE. DURING SPRING, IN THE NEIGHBOURING VILLAGE OF PUPNAT, SAGE FLOWERS SPROUT IN SUCH ABUNDANCE THAT THE HILLSIDES TURN A DAZZLING SHADE OF PURPLE.

Ingredients:

4 large zucchini (courgette)

60 grams (about ½ cup) plain flour, sifted

2 eggs, lightly beaten

handful of fresh sage leaves, finely chopped

2 tablespoons parsley, finely chopped plus extra

30 grams (1 ounce) feta cheese, crumbled (optional)

sea salt and black pepper

olive oil

- Grate zucchini and place in colander over the sink.
- Sprinkle well with salt and leave for 30 minutes to 1 hour.
- Drain zucchini, removing excess moisture by squeezing with your hands.
- Place zucchini in a bowl with sifted flour, eggs, sage, parsley, feta, salt and pepper. Mix well.
- Shallow fry spoonfuls of the mixture in oil, turning once, until fritters are golden brown on both sides.
- Serve sprinkled with the extra chopped parsley and your favourite chutney.

Lemon Marmalade

THERE ARE TWO LEMON TREES SITUATED VERY CLOSE TO OUR PROPERTY.
THE CROP ON THE MEYER IS SO PROLIFIC I NEED ONLY REACH OUT OF THE
UPSTAIRS BEDROOM WINDOW TO PICK IT.

THE SECOND TREE IS THE LISBON VARIETY AND IT IS IN THE COURTYARD
NEXT TO OUR TERRACE. THIS TREE DOESN'T BELONG TO US, ALTHOUGH WE
DO WATER IT TO ENSURE IT CONTINUES TO SURVIVE. WE ARE TOLD THAT
THE COURTYARD WHERE IT GROWS IS OWNED BY THIRTY PEOPLE, AND FROM
TIME TO TIME DIFFERENT PEOPLE APPEAR AND PICK THE CROP. MANY
SELFISHLY PICK LARGE QUANTITIES, AND WHEN I SUGGEST THEY LEAVE
SOME FOR THE OTHER OWNERS THE ANSWER IS ALWAYS THE SAME.
'WHY WOULD I DO THAT? THIS IS MY TREE.'

Ingredients:

12 large lemons

1 litre (4 cups) water

900 grams (about 4 cups) sugar

- Using a vegetable peeler, remove the rind from the lemons in strips, taking care not to include any pith as this may taint the marmalade with a bitter, unpleasant flavour.

- Cut the rind into thin, narrow strips about 2 centimetres (¾ inch) long. Cut the remaining lemon flesh into small cubes.

- If possible, remove all the pips (seeds), keeping aside a dozen. Place these in a small muslin bag secured with string and add to the marmalade during cooking.

- Place the lemon flesh and rind into a jam saucepan with the water. Cover and set aside for several hours or preferably overnight.

- Bring the lemon mixture to the boil over a high heat, stirring frequently. Reduce the heat and simmer for about 1 hour until the mixture is soft.

- Add the sugar and increase the heat to medium, stirring constantly until the sugar dissolves. Keep the mixture at a rolling boil, stirring from time to time until the marmalade becomes thick and sticky.

- Test a small amount of marmalade on a saucer chilled in the freezer. When a skin forms on the sample the marmalade is ready.

- Ladle into hot sterilized jars (see note on page 109) and seal.

Fritule

A TRADITIONAL FESTIVE TREAT. ONE OF MY CHILDHOOD DELIGHTS WAS
EATING MY GRANDMOTHER'S DELICIOUS FRITULE ALMOST STRAIGHT
FROM THE FRYING PAN AND SEVERELY REDUCING THE NUMBER LEFT TO
BE SERVED AT THE TABLE.

Ingredients:

500 grams (about 4 cups) plain flour, sifted

8 grams (1 tablespoon) fresh yeast, crumbled

pinch of salt

375 millilitres (1½ cups) milk

3 eggs, lightly beaten

3 teaspoons sugar

zest of 1 lemon

360 grams (about 2 cups) sultanas or golden raisins (soaked overnight in 60 millilitres, or ¼ cup, of rakija or rum for an extra kick)

125 millilitres (½ cup) rakija or rum, extra

sunflower oil

vanilla sugar

- Sift the flour into a large bowl. Using your fingertips, rub in the yeast. Add the salt.
- Add the milk slowly and mix to a smooth dough using a knife.
- Add the eggs, sugar, lemon zest, sultanas (or raisins) and rakija. Beat with a wooden spoon for a few minutes until smooth. The longer the dough is beaten the better the mixture will be. Cover the bowl with a baking cloth or clean tea towel. Leave in a warm place to rise for 1 hour.
- Heat the oil to medium heat in a heavy saucepan.
- Using a soup spoon dipped in oil, scoop out spoonfuls of dough, and drop 3 spoonfuls one after the other and deep fry. As soon as they begin to colour, turn with a fork to ensure they brown evenly.
- Repeat the process until all the fritule are cooked.
- Drain on kitchen paper and sprinkle with vanilla sugar.
- Serve at room temperature.

Jam Parcels

IN CROATIA THIS RECIPE IS CALLED *ROŠČIĆI* AND IS BAKED USING CREAM.
FOR MY VERSION I PREFER YOGHURT.

Ingredients:

125 grams (about ½ cup) butter, softened

150 millilitres (⅔ cup) yoghurt

200 grams (about 1½ cups) plain flour, sifted

1 heaped teaspoon baking powder

100 grams (about ¼ cup) fig jam

icing (confectioner's) sugar for dusting

- Preheat oven to 180°C (350°F).
- Mix the softened (almost melted) butter and yoghurt together well.
- Add the sifted flour and baking powder. Mix to a soft dough.
- Turn out onto a lightly floured board and knead for 5 minutes.
- Roll the dough into a thin rectangular-shaped sheet. Cut in half lengthways, before cutting each half into 12 centimetre (or 5 inch) long triangles, making about 18–20 triangles.
- Place a teaspoon of the jam at the wide end of each triangle and roll up the dough, making sure the tip of the triangle is on the underside of the parcel.
- Place on a tray lined with baking paper and bake for 15 minutes until golden brown.
- Dust with icing (confectioner's) sugar while hot.

Crystallized Peel

MOST YEARS OUR LEMON TREE PROVIDES US WITH AN EXCESS OF LEMONS, BUT THIS WAS NOT ALWAYS THE CASE. WHEN WE FIRST ARRIVED ON THE ISLAND, IF WE WENT AWAY FOR A HOLIDAY THE LOCALS WOULD COME AND STRIP OUR TREE BARE WHEN WE WERE NOT AT HOME. IT DID NOT TAKE US LONG TO REALIZE WE NEEDED A PADLOCK ON THE BACK GATE. ENJOY THESE TASTY TREATS WITH COFFEE, LIQUEURS, CHOPPED OVER DESSERTS OR IN BAKING.

Ingredients:

2 lemons and 2 oranges

1 cup white sugar

1 cup water

- Peel the lemons and oranges taking care not to include the pith. Place in a bowl and cover with water. Place in the refrigerator to soak overnight.
- Drain and slice the peel finely into 5–10 centimetre (2–4 inch) long strips.
- Prepare a baking tray, lining it with baking paper.
- In a large heavy bottomed saucepan, add the sugar and water. Stir to dissolve the sugar. Place the saucepan over high heat and bring to a rapid boil.
- After 10 minutes add the peel and stir occasionally for 15–20 minutes using a wooden spoon.
- As the mixture bubbles and becomes frothy, sugar crystals will begin to appear. Remove from the heat and continue to stir constantly. Stir steadily until the peel is coated with sugar crystals.
- Turn out the peel very quickly onto the prepared baking tray and allow to cool.
- Store in an airtight jar.

Summer

The months from June to September seem endless, with often very little or no rain and temperatures commonly reaching 35°C (95°F), at times even higher. Humidity on the coast is usually low and night time temperatures are a constant 25°C (77°F). This is the perfect time to enjoy eating *al fresco* on the terrace in the evenings. Under the intense heat of the Adriatic sun, olives and grapes begin to grow fat and ripen. The magnificent array of fresh summer vegetables from our organic garden is stunning: tomatoes, basil, zucchini (courgette), beans, capsicum (bell pepper), eggplant (aubergine), cucumber and rocket (arugula). Figs and wild blackberries are ripe for picking, and tray upon tray of figs can be seen drying on the terraces of local houses in the powerful summer sun. These will be stored for eating during the long winter months. Summer is the time for getting up early to work in the kitchen or the garden before the heat of the day arrives. Several mornings a week, usually before five o'clock, an old lady of over eighty trudges up Flower Street behind our house. With a ladder over her shoulder she heads off to toil in her olive grove.

In the height of summer, the smell of lavender is heady and strong. I harvest great bunches of the long-stemmed variety for making into lavender cages to hang in our wardrobes.

Siestas are common here in Račišće especially in summer. And what better way to escape the heat before waking up with a swim in the brilliant blue Adriatic Sea. Having shed their layers of dark winter clothing, many of the locals spend their afternoons at the beach.

Pan-Fried Eggplant (Aubergine)

EGGPLANT (AUBERGINE) IS WELL SUITED TO THE ADRIATIC CLIMATE.
ALTHOUGH THE PLANTS ARE OFTEN SLOW TO ESTABLISH THEMSELVES,
ONCE THEY BEGIN TO FLOWER, WE KNOW WE WILL ALWAYS BE ASSURED OF
AN ENDLESS CROP UNTIL THE END OF SEPTEMBER.

Ingredients:

2 tablespoons wholemeal
   (whole-wheat) flour

½ teaspoon ground cumin

½ teaspoon ground coriander

½ teaspoon ground turmeric

sea salt and black pepper

1 large eggplant (aubergine),
   cut into 1 centimetre (½
   inch) thick slices

2 tablespoons olive oil, plus
   extra

- Place flour, spices, salt and pepper into a large brown paper bag and shake to mix well. Add the eggplant slices, three at a time, and shake the bag to coat thoroughly.

- Shallow fry the eggplant slices in olive oil over medium heat for about 6 minutes on each side, shaking occasionally to ensure even frying. Continue turning until the eggplant slices are soft and golden in colour. Remove and drain on kitchen paper.

- Repeat with the remaining slices, adding a small quantity of extra oil if necessary. Do not saturate the slices while frying.

- Serve warm, drizzled with extra olive oil.

Baba Ghanoush

IT TAKES US A WEEK TO PICK OUR OLIVE TREES FOR OUR FIRST EVER
HARVEST. OUR OLIVE QUANTITY LOOKS MODEST, BUT AT THE PRESS IT
WEIGHS IN AT 116 KILOGRAMS (256 POUNDS) AND YIELDS 27 LITRES (114
CUPS) OF EXTRA VIRGIN OLIVE OIL.
WHENEVER I MAKE THIS RECIPE I ALWAYS HOPE IT WILL LAST, BUT IT
NEVER DOES. IT'S FAR TOO TASTY AND WE CANNOT RESIST ITS DISTINCTIVE
FLAVOUR.

Ingredients:

1 large eggplant (aubergine)

2 garlic cloves, crushed

¼ cup tahini

sea salt and black pepper, to season

2 tablespoons lemon juice

4 tablespoons olive oil

- Preheat the oven to 180°C (350°F).
- Cut the eggplant in half lengthwise and roast, cut side up, for 45 minutes to an hour, until very soft. Set aside to cool.
- Remove the flesh from the skin. Drain and discard any liquid.
- Place the flesh into a food processor with the remaining ingredients and blend until smooth.
- Serve on fingers of toasted wholegrain olive and rosemary bread (see recipe on page 63).
- The baba ghanoush can be stored in the refrigerator. It will keep for about a week.

Caramelized Onions

PLANTED IN AUTUMN AND HARVESTED IN SUMMER, OUR CROP OF RED ONIONS IS GROWN IN OUR FRIEND PAVO'S VINEYARD WHERE THERE IS MORE SPACE. THESE CARAMELIZED ONIONS CAN BE SERVED WITH MEAT AND CHEESE OR AS A GARNISH FOR SALAD.

Ingredients:

3 large red onions, finely sliced

2 tablespoons olive oil

1 tablespoon brown sugar

1 tablespoon balsamic vinegar

sea salt and black pepper

- Preheat the oven to 170°C (340°F).
- Place sliced onions into a large roasting dish and add olive oil, brown sugar and balsamic vinegar. Mix together until well combined. Season with salt and pepper.
- Ensure mixture is spread evenly in the roasting dish and bake for about 45 minutes, uncovered until onions are tender and just starting to brown.
- Remove from the oven and allow to cool.
- Store in the refrigerator where the caramelized onions will keep for about a week.

Slow Roasted Tomatoes

EVERY SUMMER OUR TOMATO CROP IS PROLIFIC. EACH AND EVERY VARIETY THRIVES HERE AND THE FLAVOUR IS INTENSE.

WITH HIS HABIT OF PICKING TOMATOES EARLY IN THE MORNING BEFORE THE ONSLAUGHT OF THE SUMMER HEAT, MY HUSBAND HAS BECOME A SOURCE OF AMUSEMENT TO THE LOCALS. THEY WANDER ALONG FLOWER STREET AND CALL OUT TO HIM,

'WHY YOU DO THAT? PICKING TOMATOES AND WORKING IN THE GARDEN IS WOMEN'S WORK.'

Ingredients:

tomatoes (romas are best for this recipe, but cocktail or cherry tomatoes can also be used)

olive oil

balsamic vinegar

salt and pepper

- Preheat the oven to 150°C (300°F).
- Cut the tomatoes in half horizontally and place on a large baking tray lined with baking paper.
- Drizzle with a small quantity of olive oil and balsamic vinegar. Sprinkle with salt and pepper.
- Bake for 1½ hours or until tomatoes are partially dehydrated and lightly caramelized around the edges.

Roast Red Peppers

PEČENE PAPRIKE ARE A POPULAR WAY TO EAT PEPPERS IN CROATIA. IN OUR GARDEN WE GROW ONLY THE ELONGATED RED VARIETY BECAUSE OF THEIR SWEETER FLAVOUR.

Ingredients:

6 elongated sweet red peppers

2 garlic cloves, finely sliced

1 tablespoon balsamic vinegar

2 tablespoons olive oil

salt

- Preheat the oven to 180°C (350°F).
- Cut the peppers in half lengthwise, remove the seeds and place the cut side down in a baking dish lined with baking paper.
- Brush with olive oil. Sprinkle with the garlic, balsamic vinegar and salt.
- Roast the peppers for 30 minutes until they are soft and beginning to char. The skin may be removed before eating.

Flamiche (Pizza Blanche)

TRADITIONALLY THIS IS A FRENCH RECIPE MADE WITH LEEKS AND PANCETTA. MY VERSION IS CREATED WITH CHERRY TOMATOES. EVERY SEASON OUR CHERRY TOMATO PLANTS SAG UNDER THE WEIGHT OF THEIR TRUSSES. THE TOMATOES ARE A VIBRANT RED AND BURST WITH JUICE.

Ingredients:

THE DOUGH

300 grams (about 2½ cups) plain flour

8 grams (1 tablespoon) fresh yeast, crumbled

2 teaspoons salt

tepid water to mix (see cooking notes on page 108)

THE TOPPING

1 tablespoon olive oil

1 medium red onion, finely sliced

3 eggs, lightly beaten

300 grams (about 1¼ cups) sour cream or crème fraîche

250 grams (about 1½ cups) halved cocktail or cherry tomatoes, sufficient to cover the surface of the flamiche

salt, pepper and nutmeg

gruyère cheese, grated

- Sift the flour into a large bowl and rub in the yeast using your fingertips. Add the salt.
- Add sufficient water to mix to a firm dough.
- Turn the dough out onto a lightly floured board (if you can knead without flour, so much the better). Knead the dough for 8–10 minutes until it is smooth and elastic.
- Shape the dough into a ball and place in a lightly floured bowl. Cover with a baking cloth or clean tea towel and leave to rest in a warm place for 1 hour.
- Preheat the oven to 190°C (375°F) and lightly flour a baking tray.
- Place the dough onto the baking tray. Roll the dough out, flattening it into a circle to fit the tray, making a ridge by hand around the edge to contain the filling. Set aside.
- To make the topping, heat the oil in a small frying pan and sauté the onion until soft. Set aside to cool.
- Mix together the eggs, sour cream or crème fraîche and halved tomatoes. Add the cooked onion and mix well. Season with salt, pepper and nutmeg. Spread onto the dough and scatter with grated cheese.
- Bake for 15–20 minutes until golden brown. Cool on a wire rack.

Risotto with Tomato, Basil and Lime

LIME TREES ARE SELDOM SEEN HERE. THE ONE WE HAVE CAME ALL THE WAY FROM NEW ZEALAND. I WILL NEVER FORGET TRANSPORTING THE SMALL TREE FROM AUCKLAND VIA SINGAPORE, PARIS AND LONDON. WE HAD HIDDEN IT IN THE MIDDLE OF A LARGE BUNCH OF FLOWERS TO PREVENT AIRPORT OFFICIALS QUESTIONING IT. NOW, IT IS A THRIVING TREE WHICH PRODUCES A CONSISTENT CROP OF LIMES.

Ingredients:

1 tablespoon olive oil

1 medium onion, finely sliced

2 garlic cloves, crushed

1 cup uncooked Arborio rice

500 millilitres (2 cups) chicken or vegetable stock

4 or 5 medium tomatoes, or a mixture of varieties such as roma, cherry and yellow cocktail

½ red capsicum (bell pepper), finely sliced

125 millilitres (½ cup) dry white wine

juice and zest of 1 fresh lime

1 teaspoon ground paprika

handful of fresh basil leaves

salt and green pepper

2 tablespoons parmesan cheese, grated

- Sauté the onion in olive oil in a non-stick frying pan until transparent. Add the garlic and cook 1 more minute. Add the rice and stir over medium heat for 2 minutes until rice is warm and coated with oil.
- Add the stock, tomatoes, capsicum (bell pepper), wine, lime zest, juice, paprika and most of the basil leaves, reserving a few for garnish. Stir occasionally until the mixture comes to the boil.
- Reduce the heat and simmer for about 30 minutes until rice is tender and liquid is absorbed. Stir occasionally to prevent sticking. If the mixture is too thick, add a small amount of extra stock.
- Add salt and green pepper to taste.
- Serve immediately, garnished with the parmesan cheese and basil leaves.

Shrimp Risotto

THIS CROATIAN SPECIALTY DISH CAN BE FOUND IN MANY OF THE
RESTAURANTS UP AND DOWN THE DALMATIAN COAST. THIS RECIPE WAS
SHARED WITH ME BY ONE OF THE LOCAL CHEFS FROM KONOBA VALA IN THE
VILLAGE. SITTING AT THE OUTDOOR TABLE ON MY TERRACE, OVERLOOKING
THE SEA, I OFTEN ENJOY THIS TASTY DISH WITH A GLASS OF DRY WHITE
WINE FROM THE VILLAGE OF LUMBARDA.

Ingredients:

3 tablespoons olive oil

500 grams (1 pound) fresh prawns (shrimp), peeled and deveined

1 small onion, finely diced

2 garlic cloves, crushed

1 small stick celery, finely diced

1 cup uncooked Arborio rice

125 millilitres (½ cup) dry white wine

1 tomato, blanched and skinned, seeds removed

zest from 1 lemon

750 millilitres (3 cups) heated fish or chicken stock

sea salt and black pepper, to season

grated parmesan cheese, for garnishing

chopped parsley, for garnishing

- Heat 2 tablespoons of the olive oil in a heavy-based frying pan placed over medium-high heat. Fry the prawns in hot oil, tossing frequently for about a minute until cooked. Remove from heat and set aside.

- Add the remaining oil to pan and reduce the heat to medium-low. Add onion, garlic and celery. Cook, stirring constantly, until the onion becomes transparent, about 5 minutes.

- Add the rice and stir until it is warm and coated with oil.

- Add the wine, tomato and lemon zest. Continue to stir until all the liquid has been absorbed, about 2–3 minutes.

- Add stock and continue to stir occasionally until the rice swells and absorbs all the liquid, at least 20 minutes. If the risotto becomes too dry and stock has evaporated, add boiling water, half a cup at a time, to make sure the risotto is creamy but not too wet.

- Add the prawns and heat gently for 5 more minutes on low heat. Season with salt and pepper.

- Serve immediately, sprinkled with grated parmesan cheese and chopped parsley.

Black Risotto

THIS DISH IS A MUST IF YOU HAVEN'T TRIED IT. THE TRADITIONAL CROATIAN RISOTTO, OR *CRNI RIŽOTO OD SIPE* AS IT IS CALLED IN CROATIA, IS ONE MY FAVOURITES. THE 'INK' ADDS AN UNUSUAL FLAVOUR AS WELL AS STARTLING COLOUR.

Ingredients:

1 kilogram (2¼ pounds) whole cuttlefish with ink sac intact

4 tablespoons olive oil

1 large onion, finely sliced

2 garlic cloves, crushed

3 tablespoons parsley, finely chopped

1 medium tomato, blanched, skinned and finely diced

2 tablespoons lemon juice

125 millilitres (½ cup) dry white wine

1 litre (4 cups) fish or chicken stock, heated

1½ cups uncooked Arborio rice

sea salt and black pepper

parmesan cheese, grated

extra chopped parsley

- Wash the cuttlefish under running water and pat dry with kitchen paper. Remove the dark outer skin and cartilage. Carefully take out the ink sac and reserve for using later. Slice the cuttlefish into short, thin strips.

- Sauté the onion and garlic in 2 tablespoons of olive oil, in a large heavy-based frying pan over medium heat until the onion is soft and transparent. Be careful not to burn the garlic.

- Add the cuttlefish, parsley, tomato, lemon juice, wine and a small amount of stock. Continue to simmer until the cuttlefish becomes tender. Remove from the heat and set aside.

- Heat the remaining olive oil in a frying pan over medium heat. Add rice and stir for 2 minutes until the rice is warm and coated with oil.

- Add the remainder of the stock and continue to cook for 20–30 more minutes until the rice is creamy and tender and liquid has been absorbed. Stir occasionally. Add boiling water if the risotto becomes too dry.

- Remove rice mixture from the heat and carefully add the contents of the ink sac. Stir to mix well.

- Add the reserved cuttlefish to the rice mixture and heat gently for 5 minutes.

- Season to taste.

- Serve immediately, garnished with the parmesan cheese and the extra chopped parsley.

Scampi Buzara

IN ITALY, PRAWNS (SHRIMP) FROM THE ADRIATIC ARE KNOWN AS SCAMPI.
THIS RECIPE FOR PRAWN STEW WAS GIVEN TO ME BY ZVON, MY CROATIAN
CHEF FRIEND FROM ZAGREB. WE ENJOYED A SUPERB *AL FRESCO* DINNER ON
HIS TERRACE LATE ONE SUMMER'S NIGHT UNDER THE MOON AND THE STARS.
ALTHOUGH THIS DISH WAS MESSY TO EAT, THE FLAVOUR WAS EXCEPTIONAL.

Ingredients:

4 tablespoons olive oil

2 garlic cloves, crushed

¼ cup fresh breadcrumbs

4–5 tomatoes, skinned and diced

2 tablespoons lemon juice

250 millilitres (1 cup) dry white wine

1 kilogram (2¼ pounds) fresh scampi,
   peeled and deveined

sea salt and black pepper

200 grams (7 ounces) dried spaghetti

2 tablespoons parsley, finely chopped

fresh bread

- Heat the olive oil in a heavy-based saucepan over medium heat. Add the garlic and breadcrumbs. Sauté for 1–2 minutes until light golden brown.
- Add the tomatoes, lemon juice and wine. Simmer for 10 minutes.
- Put on water to boil in saucepan large enough to cook the spaghetti.
- Add scampi to the saucepan with the tomatoes, cover and simmer for 10 minutes until the sauce has thickened and reduced slightly. Season to taste.
- Cook the spaghetti in the boiling water until al dente.
- Once the pasta is cooked, serve the sauce over the top of the spaghetti. Sprinkle with chopped parsley and serve with crusty, fresh baked bread to soak up the sauce.

Fig Flan

FIGS ARE WITHOUT A DOUBT MY FAVOURITE FRUIT OF THE LAND IN
RAČIŠĆE. THIS RECIPE ORIGINATED IN BRITTANY WHERE THIS FLAN IS
TRADITIONALLY BAKED WITH PRUNES.

Ingredients:

400 grams (about 2½ cups) poached
  glazed figs (see recipe on page 45)

50 millilitres (3–4 tablespoons) rakija
  or rum

30 grams (2 tablespoons) butter,
  melted

130 grams (about ⅔ cup) sugar

4 large eggs

110 grams (about 1 cup) plain flour,
  sifted

pinch of salt

750 millilitres (3 cups) full-cream milk

- In a medium-sized glass or ceramic bowl, soak the figs in alcohol for a few hours or overnight if possible.

- Preheat the oven to 190°C (375°F). Brush a medium baking dish, approximately 30 x 20 centimetre (8 x 12 inch), with the melted butter.

- Beat the sugar and eggs together until light and frothy.

- Add the flour gradually, followed by the salt.

- Whisk in the cold milk to make a thin batter.

- Drain the figs and spoon them into the buttered dish and warm in the oven for a few minutes. Remove from the oven and pour over the batter.

- Bake for 10 minutes before reducing the heat to 180°C (350°F) for 25–30 more minutes. To check if the flan is cooked, dip the blade of a sharp knife into cold water and pierce the centre. If the knife comes out clean, it is cooked.

Glazed Figs

HOW LUCKY WE ARE TO HAVE A CHOICE OF FOUR DIFFERENT VARIETIES
OF FIGS. THE LARGE BELL-SHAPED BLACK VARIETY, WHICH RIPENS LAST,
HAS THE MOST INTENSE FLAVOUR. IT IS BY FAR THE BEST FIG FOR THE
FOLLOWING RECIPE BECAUSE THE SKIN REMAINS FIRM DURING COOKING.

Ingredients:

1 kilogram (2¼ pounds) ripe figs

3 lemons

2 cinnamon sticks

1 teaspoon whole cloves

3 tablespoons ground ginger or 50
  grams fresh ginger, finely diced

1½ cups water

700 grams (about 3½ cups) sugar

- Prepare the figs by removing the stems and cutting a small cross into the base of each.
- Slice the lemons thinly.
- In a large saucepan, place the figs, lemon slices, cinnamon sticks, cloves, ginger and water.
- Place over medium heat and bring to the boil. Reduce the heat to low and simmer for 5 minutes.
- Add the sugar gradually and simmer over a low heat until figs and lemons have become glassy and the syrup is thick. This will take about an hour and a half.
- Ladle into hot sterilized jars (see note on page 109) and seal.

Spiced Fig and Basil Jam

I NEVER EXPERIENCE A SHORTAGE OF BASIL HERE AS THE CLIMATE IS
PERFECT FOR GROWING IT IN ABUNDANCE.
IT HASN'T TAKEN LONG FOR WORD TO GET AROUND THE VILLAGE THAT I
MAKE JAM, AND NOW AS SOON AS THE FIGS ARE RIPE, LOCALS TURN UP ON MY
DOORSTEP CARRYING FIGS, JARS AND SUGAR. I CAN'T BELIEVE THEY DON'T
KNOW HOW TO MAKE JAM. ARE THEY LAZY? OR COULD IT BE THAT THEY
PREFER THE FLAVOUR OF MINE TO THEIRS?

Ingredients:

1 kilogram (2¼ pounds) ripe figs,
    quartered with stalks removed

750 millilitres (3 cups) water

500 grams (about 2½ cups) sugar

handful basil leaves, finely chopped

1 teaspoon ground cinnamon

zest and juice from 1 lemon

½ teaspoon ground cloves

- Place the figs and water in a jam or large saucepan and bring to the boil. Reduce the heat to low and simmer until the figs are soft.
- Add the sugar and stir until it is dissolved. Add the remainder of the ingredients and bring to the boil.
- Boil until thick and sticky.
- Test a small amount of jam on a saucer that has been chilled in the freezer. When a skin forms on the sample, the jam is ready.
- Ladle into hot sterilized jars (see note on page 109) and seal.

Tomato Chutney

SPICES FROM AN ANCIENT STALL IN THE SARAJEVO MARKETPLACE TRANSFORM OUR GARDEN VEGETABLES INTO A TANGY CHUTNEY WITH A FRAGRANT AROMA.

Ingredients:

6 medium to large tomatoes, coarsely chopped

½ teaspoon salt

3 medium to large elongated red capsicums (sweet peppers), finely diced

120 grams (about ⅔ cup) brown sugar

1 jalapeno (optional), finely diced

120 millilitres (½ cup) red wine vinegar

1 medium onion, cut into 2 centimetre (¾ inch) long thin slices

180 grams (about 1 cup) raisins or sultanas

3 garlic cloves, crushed

30 grams (about 2 tablespoons) fresh ginger, finely sliced

½ teaspoon ground cinnamon

½ teaspoon ground cumin

½ teaspoon ground turmeric

½ teaspoon ground allspice

- Place all ingredients into a jam or large saucepan over medium to high heat. Stir until the mixture boils.
- Reduce the heat to low and simmer for 45–60 minutes until the chutney becomes thick. Stir occasionally to prevent sticking.
- Ladle into hot sterilized jars (see note on page 109) and seal.

Fresh Fig Chutney

WHEN THE VILLAGE BECOMES CLOGGED WITH THE OVERPOWERING STENCH
OF BURNING SULPHUR WE KNOW THE LOCALS HAVE BEGUN THE PROCESS OF
DRYING FIGS.
THEIR STERILIZATION METHOD IS TO PLACE RACKS OF FIGS IN AN OLD DRUM
WITH BURNING SULPHUR IN THE BOTTOM OF IT. ONCE THIS PROCESS IS
COMPLETE, THE FIGS ARE WASHED IN SALT WATER BEFORE BEING STACKED
IN SINGLE LAYERS ON TRAYS TO DRY IN THE SUN.

Ingredients:

700 grams (1½ pounds) ripe figs,
   quartered with stalks removed

zest from half a lemon

600 millilitres (2½ cups) red wine
   vinegar

2 teaspoons yellow mustard seeds

225 grams (about 1 cup) brown sugar

30 grams (about 2 tablespoons) fresh
   ginger, finely sliced

1 onion, finely sliced

1 teaspoon salt

1 cinnamon stick

½ teaspoon ground allspice

½ teaspoon ground cloves (or 6 cloves
   in a muslin cooking bag)

- Place all ingredients into a jam or large saucepan over medium to high heat. Stir until the mixture boils.
- Reduce the heat to low and simmer until the mixture is thick and sticky, and the figs are falling apart, about 45 minutes. Remove the cinnamon stick and clove-filled muslin bag.
- Ladle into hot sterilized jars (see note on page 109) and seal.

Fig and Rocket (Arugula) Salad

ROCKET (ARUGULA) IS AN EXCELLENT SPRING AND AUTUMN CROP HERE IN RAČIŠĆE. WE GROW ROTATIONAL CROPS, PLANTING SEEDS EVERY THREE WEEKS. ITS SPICY FLAVOUR IS A GREAT ADDITION TO THIS UNUSUAL SALAD.

Ingredients:

large handful of baby rocket (arugula) leaves

8–10 fresh ripe figs, stalks removed

6 tablespoons olive oil

3 tablespoons lemon juice

1 tablespoon liquid honey

6 slices of pršut, pancetta or crisply fried bacon

mozzarella or pecorino cheese or a combination of both

basil leaves

sea salt and black pepper

- Place the rocket (arugula) in a salad bowl. Cut a cross in the bottom of each fig to allow the dressing to penetrate and place figs on top of the rocket (arugula) leaves.
- To make the dressing, whisk together the olive oil, lemon juice and honey.
- Add the slices of pršut, cheese and basil leaves to the salad and drizzle with the dressing.
- Season to taste.

Fresh Pasta with Summer Vegetables

TO MAKE THIS RECIPE, YOU WILL NEED A PASTA MACHINE. IN OUR BACKYARD THERE IS A RUSTY OLD SHIP'S BOILER. IT IS UNSIGHTLY AND BECAUSE WE CANNOT REMOVE IT WITHOUT TOO MUCH EFFORT OR EXPENSE, I DECIDED THE BEST SOLUTION WOULD BE TO DISGUISE IT BY FILLING IT WITH HERBS. AROUND THE OUTSIDE I PLANTED HANGING ROSEMARY, AND IN THE CENTRE, BASIL, OREGANO, MARJORAM, SAGE AND THYME. SITUATED IN THE FULL SUN FOR MOST OF THE DAY, THESE HERBS ARE LUSH AND PLENTIFUL.

Ingredients:

220 grams (about 1¾ cups) plain flour

80 grams (about ½ cup) coarse semolina

2 eggs

60 millilitres (¼ cup) iced water

400 grams (14 ounces) halved cherry or cocktail tomatoes

2 handfuls combination of fresh basil, marjoram and/or baby rocket (arugula)

4 tablespoons olive oil

1 large garlic clove, crushed

2 tablespoons balsamic vinegar

salt and green pepper

grated parmesan cheese or aged cheddar

- Place the flour and semolina in a food processor and pulse until combined. Keeping the motor running, add the eggs followed by the iced water. Process until the mixture just comes together.

- Remove from the food processor and knead the dough until smooth. Wrap in plastic food wrap and refrigerate for up to 3 hours.

- Remove the dough from the refrigerator, flatten and dust lightly with flour.

- With the pasta machine rollers at the widest setting, feed the dough through the rollers. Fold dough in half lengthways and feed through rollers again. Repeat until smooth, reducing roller settings notch by notch until dough is 1 centimetre (⅓ inch) thick. Pasta may need to be coated lightly with flour during rolling process if it becomes sticky.

- Finally, put dough through desired machine setting for either spaghetti or fettuccine. Leave pasta to dry for at least 3 hours before cooking.

- Place pasta in a large pan of salted, boiling water and cook until al dente. Fresh pasta will take longer to cook than dried pasta, about 15 minutes.

- While pasta is cooking, place the halved tomatoes in a bowl. Add the herbs, olive oil, garlic and vinegar. Season to taste and stir gently to combine. Set aside.

- Drain the pasta and while it is hot, mix through the tomato mixture.

- Serve sprinkled with freshly grated parmesan cheese or aged chedar.

Fresh Fig Crumble

WHENEVER I EAT FIGS I AM ALWAYS TRANSPORTED BACK TO MY CHILDHOOD
AND SUMMER AT MY GRANDMOTHER'S HOUSE. IN HER GARDEN THERE
WAS AN ENORMOUS FIG TREE WHERE, DURING THE HEAT OF SUMMER,
MY BROTHERS AND I HID IN THE SHADE AND GORGED OURSELVES ON
SUCCULENT JUICY FIGS. WE THOUGHT WE WOULD NOT BE FOUND OUT, BUT
OUR STICKY FINGERS AND SMEARY FACES INVARIABLY GAVE US AWAY.

Ingredients:

120 grams (about 1 cup) flour (wholemeal/whole-wheat/white/rye)

90 grams (about 6 tablespoons) butter, cut into small cubes

100 grams (about ½ cup) brown sugar

300 grams (about 10½ ounces) ripe figs, quartered with stalks removed

125 millilitres (½ cup) water

1 teaspoon ground cinnamon

- Preheat the oven to 180°C (350°F). Grease a medium-sized baking dish.
- Place the flour and butter in a food processor and pulse until the mixture resembles breadcrumbs.
- Add the sugar and pulse briefly to mix.
- Layer the figs in the baking dish. Pour over the water and cover with the crumble mixture.
- Sprinkle with cinnamon.
- Bake for 30–40 minutes or until golden brown.

Roast Zucchini (Courgette) with Lemon and Mint

ALTHOUGH THEY ARE EASY TO GROW IN RAČIŠĆE, ZUCCHINI (COURGETTE) REQUIRE PLENTY OF WATERING. FOR THIS REASON THE LOCALS DON'T PLANT THEM ON A REGULAR BASIS BECAUSE THEIR GARDEN PLOTS ARE USUALLY 500 METRES (⅓ OF A MILE) OR MORE AWAY FROM THEIR HOUSES WHERE NO WATER SUPPLY IS AVAILABLE.

Ingredients:

4 zucchini (courgette)

balsamic vinegar

2 tablespoons fresh mint, finely chopped

2 tablespoons lemon zest

olive oil

sea salt and black pepper

- Preheat the oven to 180°C (350°F). Line a baking dish with baking paper.
- Cut the zucchini in half and slice lengthways. Slices should be thin. Place in the baking dish.
- Sprinkle with balsamic vinegar, top with mint, lemon zest and drizzle with olive oil. Season with salt and pepper.
- Roast for about 30 minutes until zucchini are soft and starting to colour.

Lemon and Lavender Shortbread

IN THE STONY SOIL AND UNDER THE INTENSE HEAT OF THE ADRIATIC SUN LAVENDER PLANTS THRIVE. IN MY GARDEN I HAVE TWENTY-TWO HEALTHY SPECIMENS. I USED TO HAVE TWENTY-THREE UNTIL THE GRUMPY OLD LADY NEXT DOOR DECIDED I HAD PLANTED ONE PLANT TOO CLOSE TO HER BOUNDARY. SOUNDLESSLY, DURING THE MIDDLE OF THE NIGHT, SHE PUT A RING OF RUSTY NAILS IN THE SOIL AROUND THIS PLANT. EVERY DAY I REMOVED THEM, AND EVERY NIGHT SHE PUT THEM BACK, UNTIL IN THE END THE PLANT SUCCUMBED, TURNED UP ITS TOES AND DIED.

Ingredients:

250 grams (about 1 cup) softened butter

125 grams (about 1 cup) icing (confectioner's) sugar

250 grams (about 2 cups) plain flour

125 grams (about 1 cup) cornflour

zest from 1 lemon

2 tablespoons lavender flowers, finely chopped

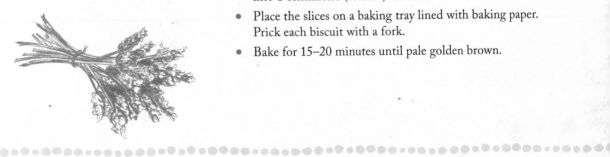

- Cream the butter and icing (confectioner's) sugar until light and fluffy.
- Sift the flour and cornflour together. Add to the creamed mixture.
- Add the lemon zest and lavender. Knead well.
- Divide the dough into 2 equal portions and shape into 2 logs, about 18–20 centimetre (7–8 inches) long.
- Wrap in plastic food wrap and refrigerate for 1 hour.
- Preheat the oven to 180°C (350°F).
- Remove the logs from the fridge, unwrap and cut each log into 1 centimetre (⅓ inch) slices.
- Place the slices on a baking tray lined with baking paper. Prick each biscuit with a fork.
- Bake for 15–20 minutes until pale golden brown.

Zucchini (Courgette) Bread

EVERY YEAR WE HAVE A SURPLUS OF ZUCCHINI (COURGETTE).
WITH A NUTTY, MOIST SAVOURY FLAVOUR, THIS LOAF FREEZES WELL
AND THAWS QUICKLY IN THE MICROWAVE.

Ingredients:

4 eggs

200 grams (about 1 cup) brown sugar

250 millilitres (1 cup) olive oil

250 millilitres (1 cup) water

2 teaspoons vanilla

440 grams (about 3½ cups) self-raising flour

1 teaspoon cinnamon

1 teaspoon four spice

1 teaspoon nutmeg

pinch of salt

2 cups grated zucchini (courgette)

½ teaspoon baking soda

120 grams (about 1 cup) walnuts, roughly chopped

180 grams (about 1 cup) raisins

- Preheat the oven to 170°C (340°F). Grease 2 loaf tins — approximately 28 x 12 centimetres (5 x 11 inches).
- Beat together the eggs and brown sugar in a large bowl.
- Add the oil, water, vanilla, flour, spices and salt.
- Stir in the grated zucchini, baking soda, walnuts and raisins.
- Divide evenly between the two loaf tins and smooth the tops.
- Bake for 40–60 minutes until golden brown. Test with a skewer. When inserted into the cake it should come out clean.
- Cool for 10 minutes before removing from the tins.

Biscotti

How many times have I tried to eat a green almond? Sufficient to know I will never acquire a taste for them. Every year our friend Paulina delights in telling me how much she loves the bitter taste of the furry fruits and how she prefers it to the taste of ripe ones.

Ingredients:

250 grams (about 2 cups) plain flour

2 teaspoons baking powder

pinch of salt

150 grams (about ¾ cup) sugar

3 eggs

zest from 2 lemons

60 grams (about ½ cup) roasted almonds, roughly chopped

- Preheat the oven to 180°C (350°F).
- Sift the flour, baking powder and salt into a bowl. Add the sugar.
- Beat together the eggs and lemon zest.
- Add the egg mixture to the dry ingredients along with the almonds and mix to a firm dough. Add more flour if necessary.
- Shape into a log about 30 centimetres (1 foot) long. Place on a baking tray lined with baking paper and flatten the log slightly with the palm of your hand. The log should be oval shaped rather than round.
- Bake for about 35 minutes or until cooked. Allow to cool for 10 minutes before cutting the log into 1 centimetre (⅓ inch) slices on the diagonal.
- Return the biscotti to the baking tray, reduce the heat to 150°C (300°F) and bake for 20 more minutes or until the biscotti are dry and crisp. Cool on the tray.
- The biscotti can be stored in an airtight container.

Autumn

Autumn is harvest season for both grapes and olives. It is also my absolute favourite time of year in Račišće. From mid September until November the days and nights are comfortably cool as the weather remains settled. In mid September, wine barrels appear on the village waterfront where they are filled with sea water to swell the timber and close the cracks. In the latter half of September, it is traditional for many families to make wine in their *konobas* (wine cellars). Almonds and walnuts are harvested and stored for eating during winter. Squid are at their most abundant in the sea at this time of year and the best fishing is at dawn, or more particularly, dusk. As the lemon trees begin to recover from the heat of summer, which often wilts and curls their leaves, yellow crocus flowers pop up in village gardens, fields and along the edges of pathways. Once the last of the summer vegetables have been harvested, it's time to plant potatoes, garlic and onions before the olive harvest in November takes place. November is often dry, but there can be heavy rain and the threat of this makes it difficult to decide when to harvest the olives. Although it is ideal is to harvest them at the peak of their ripeness, if heavy rain is likely, then it is important to pick before the rain soaks and ruins the crop by filling the olives with water.

Basil Pesto

I LOVE PESTO. AT THE TIME OF COMPILING THIS BOOK IT WAS A BUMPER
SEASON FOR ALMONDS. YOU NEVER KNOW WHAT EACH SEASON WILL BRING;
THE PREVIOUS YEAR THE CROP WAS ALMOST NON-EXISTENT. THE INTENSE
NUTTY FLAVOUR OF FRESHLY ROASTED ALMONDS, TOGETHER WITH
BASIL AND FRESHLY GROUND GREEN PEPPERCORNS FROM SARAJEVO, IS
MAGNIFICENT.

- Place the basil in a colander and pour boiling water over it.
  Then place under cold running water immediately to prevent
  excess wilting.
- Place the almonds, walnuts or pinenuts in a food processor
  and grind until fine.
- Squeeze the excess water from the basil, then add the basil
  to the food processor with the remaining ingredients. Pulse
  until smooth.
- Store in a sterilized jar (see note on page 109) in the
  refrigerator with a thin layer of oil covering the top to
  prevent oxidization and discolouration.

Ingredients:

2 large handfuls of basil, coarse stalks
    removed

2 tablespoons toasted almonds,
    walnuts or pinenuts

salt and green pepper

3 large garlic cloves, sliced

125 millilitres (½ cup) olive oil

30 grams (about 1 ounce) parmesan
    cheese, grated

Olives in Brine

THERE ARE TWENTY TREES IN THE THREE OLIVE GROVES WE WORK. FROM
YEAR TO YEAR THE CROP VARIES DEPENDING ON THE WIND, SUN AND
RAIN. LAST YEAR WE EXPERIENCED THE WORST OLIVE SEASON WE HAVE
ENCOUNTERED HERE SO FAR. THE FLOWERS WERE IN THE PROCESS OF
SETTING WHEN THE WIND BLEW CONTINUOUSLY AND HEAVY RAIN FELL.
THE RESULT WAS DISASTROUS AND PRODUCED AN EXTREMELY POOR, ALMOST
NON-EXISTENT CROP. A NUMBER OF THE VILLAGE PEOPLE DID NOT EVEN
HARVEST THEIR OLIVES, LET ALONE PRESS THE OIL. WE USUALLY ACHIEVE
SOMEWHERE IN THE VICINITY OF 35 LITRES (148 CUPS) OF THICK RICH OIL,
BUT THIS SEASON WE PRESSED A MERE 7 LITRES (29 CUPS). BUT ALL WAS
NOT LOST, AND WITH THE PERMISSION OF THE OWNERS WE HARVESTED THE
OLIVES FROM UNWANTED TREES AND MARINATED THEM, USING THIS RECIPE.

Ingredients:

**1 kilogram (2¼ pounds)
fresh ripe black olives,
stalks removed**

coarse rock or sea salt

olive oil

FOR THE BRINE

**100 grams (about ½ cup)
salt per litre (about 4
cups) of water**

- Place the washed olives in a large non-corrosive dish (ceramic or glass), sprinkle heavily with the coarse salt, mix well and leave overnight.
- The next day, drain away the accumulated liquid. Add another sprinkling of salt and leave again to marinate overnight. Repeat this procedure for 5 days.
- On the sixth day, rinse the olives well in several changes of water before making the brine.
- For the brine, place the water in a large saucepan, bring to the boil and add the salt, using the ratios in the ingredients list. Stir until dissolved.
- Pack olives into warm, sterilized jars (see note on page 109) and fill with the hot brine. Top with a thin layer of oil to keep the olives submerged. Seal the jars and leave for a minimum of four months in a cool place.
- After four months or longer, drain and rinse the olives well before storing in olive oil. At this stage, flavourings such as garlic, lemon, rosemary or chilli (chili pepper) may be added.
- Store in the refrigerator in screwtop jars.

Tapenade

IN AND AROUND RAČIŠĆE, THERE ARE BETWEEN 30,000 AND 40,000 OLIVE
TREES, ALL PLANTED DURING THE LAST 300 YEARS. AS A RESULT OF THE
DECLINING VILLAGE POPULATION, TODAY, LESS THAN 10 PER CENT OF THESE
MAJESTIC TREES ARE MAINTAINED AND HARVESTED.
TAPENADE IS A DELICIOUS SNACK SPREAD ON TOASTED WHOLEGRAIN OLIVE
AND ROSEMARY BREAD (SEE PAGE 63).

Ingredients:

135 grams (about 1 cup) pitted black
olives

1 tablespoon capers

2 garlic cloves, crushed

2 salted anchovies (optional)

2 tablespoons olive oil

1 tablespoon lemon juice

black pepper

- Place the olives, capers, garlic and anchovies in a food
processor and pulse until combined.
- With the motor running, pour in the olive oil until the
mixture forms a soft, textured paste. Do not over-process, as
the tapenade should not be too smooth.
- Stir in the lemon juice and season to taste with the pepper.
- Store covered in the refrigerator. Tapenade will keep for
about a week.

Wholegrain Olive and Rosemary Bread

ROSEMARY ALSO GROWS HERE IN ABUNDANCE. ITS FLOWERING PERIOD IS LONG AND THE SIGHT OF THE BUSHES SMOTHERED WITH BRIGHT BLUE FLOWERS AGAINST A BACKDROP OF DEEP GREEN LEAVES GROWING ADJACENT TO FLOWER STREET IS STUNNING.
A DENSE, MOIST LOAF WITH ENORMOUS FLAVOUR AND A THICK CRUST, THIS IS MY FAVOURITE BREAD.

Ingredients:

240 grams (about 2 cups) plain flour

120 grams (about 1 cup) wholemeal (whole-wheat) or rye flour

8 grams (1 tablespoon) fresh yeast, crumbled

handful of rosemary, finely chopped

15 pitted black olives, sliced

2 tablespoons sunflower seeds

2 tablespoons sesame seeds

2 tablespoons linseeds (flaxseeds)

2 tablespoons pumpkin seeds

2 tablespoons ground espresso coffee (to add colour)

1 tablespoon olive oil

2 teaspoons salt

tepid water to mix (see cooking notes on page 108)

- Sift the flours into a large mixing bowl. Rub in the yeast using your fingertips. Add the rosemary, olives, seeds, coffee, olive oil and finally the salt.

- Add sufficient water and mix to a firm dough.

- Turn the dough out onto a lightly floured work surface. Knead the dough for 8 minutes until it is smooth and elastic.

- Shape the dough into a ball and place in a lightly floured bowl. Cover with a baking cloth or clean tea towel and leave to rise in a warm place for 1 hour.

- Remove from the bowl and re-shape into a loaf on a lightly floured work surface, kneading the dough to make a spine or seam on the underside.

- Place on a baking tray dusted with flour and leave in a warm place for 1 more hour.

- Preheat the oven to 200°C (390°F). Score the top of the loaf with 3 diagonal cuts. Make the cuts swiftly and cleanly with a sharp knife. Do not pull or drag the dough.

- Bake for 25 minutes until the loaf is golden brown and sounds hollow when tapped. Cool on a wire rack.

End of Summer Calzone

A GREAT USE FOR THE END OF SUMMER VEGETABLES WHICH ARE OFTEN NOT
AS PERFECT AS THOSE HARVESTED DURING THE PEAK OF THE SEASON.

Ingredients:

THE DOUGH

400 grams (about 3 cups) plain flour

8 grams (1 tablespoon) fresh yeast, crumbled

2 tablespoons olive oil, plus extra

2 teaspoons salt

tepid water to mix (see cooking notes on page 108)

THE FILLING

2 tablespoons olive oil, plus extra

1 onion, finely sliced

3 garlic cloves, crushed

1 medium zucchini (courgette), sliced

1 medium eggplant (aubergine), diced

4 medium tomatoes, diced

125 millilitres (½ cup) dry white wine

sea salt and black pepper

handful of fresh rocket (arugula) leaves

90 grams (about ¾ cup) parmesan cheese or aged cheddar, grated

handful of fresh basil leaves

extra olive oil

- Sift the flour into a large bowl and rub in the yeast using your fingertips. Add the olive oil and salt.

- Add sufficient water and mix to a firm dough.

- Turn the dough out onto a lightly floured board (if you can knead without flour, so much the better). Knead the dough for 8 minutes until it is smooth.

- Shape the dough into a ball and place in a lightly floured bowl. Cover with a baking cloth or tea towel and leave to rise in a warm place for 1 hour, until almost doubled in size.

- Meanwhile, prepare the filling. In a large frying pan over medium heat, heat the olive oil and fry the onion, garlic, zucchini and eggplant, stirring frequently. Once onion is transparent and vegetables are starting to colour, add the tomatoes and wine. Bring to the boil, reduce the heat and simmer for about 1 hour or until the mixture is well cooked, thick and holds its shape. Season to taste and allow to cool.

- Preheat the oven to 200°C (390°F).

- Remove the dough from the bowl and cut into 4 pieces. Re-shape each piece into a ball on a lightly floured work surface. Roll and flatten each ball into a circle about the size of a large bread and butter plate.

- Place a thin layer of rocket (arugula) and cheese on each round, slightly off centre, and cover first with 2 tablespoons of the vegetable mixture followed by basil leaves and another thin layer of cheese. Fold the rounds in half, pushing together the edges and sealing with your fingertips. Place in a baking dish lined with baking paper. This is to catch the filling which may bubble out during cooking.

- Leave to rest for 10 minutes.

- Brush the dough with extra olive oil and score the top of each calzone with 3 angled cuts.

- Bake for 20 minutes until golden brown. Allow to cool before serving.

Stuffed Peppers

PUNJENE PAPRIKE IS NOT ONLY A TRADITIONAL CROATIAN DISH BUT ONE
THAT IS VERY COMMON IN THIS VILLAGE. IT IS USUALLY MADE WITH THE
PALE GREEN VARIETY OF PEPPERS WHICH ARE THE TRADITIONAL VARIETY
GROWN HERE. THE MINCED MEAT THE LOCAL PEOPLE USE FOR THIS RECIPE
IS MORE OFTEN THAN NOT A MIXTURE OF LAMB, BEEF AND PORK. THE MEAT IS
HIGH QUALITY AND RELATIVELY FAT FREE AND THE COMBINATION ADDS
SIGNIFICANTLY TO THE FLAVOUR OF THIS DISH.

Ingredients:

8 capsicums (bell peppers), any colour

3 tablespoons olive oil

1 onion, finely sliced

350 grams (12 ounces) lean minced beef

100 grams (3½ ounces) pancetta or bacon, diced

2 garlic cloves, crushed

1 tablespoon rosemary, finely chopped

1 cup uncooked long-grain rice

sea salt and black pepper, to season

1 egg, beaten

2 cups tomatoes, skinned and puréed

125 millilitres (½ cup) dry white wine

2 bay leaves

1 tablespoon chopped parsley

- Cut the tops off the capsicums (bell peppers) and remove the seeds.
- Heat the oil in a heavy-based frying pan. Fry the onion until soft. Add the minced meat, bacon, garlic and rosemary. Fry for 8 more minutes over medium heat until the mince is browned.
- Add the rice and cook over low heat for 5 more minutes. Add the salt and pepper to taste. Cool.
- Add the egg and fill the capsicums (bell peppers) with the mixture, but not too tightly as the rice will expand during cooking.
- Arrange the capsicums (bell peppers) in a large saucepan. Pour over the tomato purée and the white wine. Add the bay leaves and parsley. Bring to the boil. Reduce heat to low, and simmer covered for 1 hour. Do not stir.
- Serve hot.

Spiced Lentils with Roast Cherry Tomatoes and Shallots

I WAS INSPIRED TO MAKE THIS RECIPE WITH AN ITALIAN INFLUENCE WHEN
WE CAME UPON LENTILS GROWING WILD IN OUR OLIVE GROVE AT GLAVA.

Ingredients:

10 shallots

12 cherry or cocktail tomatoes

4 tablespoons olive oil

salt and green pepper

1 cup uncooked lentils, any variety

750 millilitres (3 cups) water

1 teaspoon ground cumin

1 teaspoon ground turmeric

2 teaspoons mustard seeds

2 tablespoons grated fresh ginger

250 millilitres (1 cup) coconut milk

- Preheat the oven to 200°C (390°F).
- Peel the shallots and place with the tomatoes into a baking dish lined with baking paper. Drizzle with olive oil and season with salt and freshly ground green pepper.
- Bake for 30 minutes until shallots begin to turn brown and the tomatoes are splitting. Remove from the oven and set aside.
- Place the lentils in a saucepan with 3 cups of cold water and bring to the boil. Reduce the heat to low and simmer for about 30 minutes until lentils are soft. Remove from the heat, drain and set aside.
- Heat the remaining olive oil in a heavy-based frying pan over a medium heat. Add the cumin, turmeric and mustard seeds and cook covered until the mustard seeds begin to pop. Stir occasionally. Add the ginger and continue to cook for 1 minute.
- Add the lentils, coconut milk, tomatoes and shallots. Stir gently and simmer for 5 minutes until combined.
- Serve hot.

Roast Tomato and Red Capsicum (Bell Pepper) Soup

SOUP IS A GREAT WAY TO WARM UP ON A COLD AUTUMN DAY SPENT HARVESTING OLIVES. AT LUNCHTIME WE BASK IN THE AUTUMN SUN UNDER THE SPREADING BRANCHES OF ONE OF OUR OLDER, MORE SUBSTANTIAL OLIVE TREES AND ENJOY A THERMOS OF THIS UNUSUAL SOUP TOGETHER WITH A WARM LOAF OF ROSEMARY AND OLIVE BREAD, BAKED EARLIER IN THE DAY.

Ingredients:

3 red capsicums (bell peppers), deseeded and sliced

6 roma tomatoes, diced

1 large red onion, finely sliced

3 garlic cloves, crushed

1 teaspoon ground cumin

1 teaspoon smoked paprika

2 tablespoons olive oil

750 millilitres (3 cups) vegetable stock

2 teaspoons balsamic vinegar

basil leaves for garnish

- Preheat the oven to 190°C (375°F).
- Place the capsicums (bell peppers), tomatoes, onion, garlic and cumin in a baking dish lined with baking paper and sprinkle with the smoked paprika and olive oil. Roast for 35–40 minutes until soft.
- Remove from the oven and place in a large saucepan with the vegetable stock.
- Bring to the boil and simmer for 15 minutes.
- Purée the vegetable mixture in a blender and return to the saucepan. Add balsamic vinegar.
- Serve warm and garnish with basil leaves.

Leeks and Tomatoes in White Wine Sauce

LEEKS ARE EASY AND REWARDING VEGETABLES TO GROW. THIS DISH IS AN EXCEPTIONAL ACCOMPANIMENT TO ANY FISH, MEAT OR CHICKEN.

Ingredients:

4 leeks

2 tablespoons butter

2 tablespoons olive oil

6 medium tomatoes, diced

185 millilitres (¾ cup) dry white wine

sea salt and green pepper

- Rinse the leeks well and trim off the coarse green tops. Slice lengthwise and rinse a second time. Slice thinly crossways.
- Place frying pan over medium heat. Add butter, olive oil and leeks and fry gently until soft.
- Add the tomatoes, wine, salt and green pepper. Simmer for 20–30 minutes until the mixture thickens.

Olive and Lemon Chicken

THYME IS DIFFICULT TO GROW IN THIS HOT, DRY CLIMATE. IT IS BEST SUITED TO A SEMI-SHADE AREA BECAUSE IT HAS A TENDENCY TO DRY OUT EASILY DURING THE LONG HOT SUMMER IF IT IS NOT WELL WATERED.

Ingredients:

2 large garlic cloves

2 tablespoons roughly chopped thyme

2 tablespoons lemon juice

80 millilitres (⅓ cup) olive oil

3 lemons, thinly sliced

8 boneless chicken pieces

15 black olives

- Bruise the garlic and thyme in mortar with pestle. Add the lemon juice and olive oil.
- Place the lemon slices on the base of a casserole dish, add the chicken in a single layer and pour the garlic mixture over it. Season with salt and pepper and turn to coat. Cover and stand for an hour.
- Add the olives.
- Preheat the oven to 200°C (390°F). Roast, covered, for 20–30 minutes or until the juice runs clear when chicken is tested with a skewer.

Roast Chicken with Pršut

THIS IS A TRADITIONAL CROATIAN WAY TO COOK CHICKEN.
THIS YEAR OUR QUANTITIES OF PARSLEY WERE SO PLENTIFUL THAT WE HAVE
BEGUN DOING WHAT THE LOCALS DO — FREEZING THE HERB IN PLASTIC
BAGS. I WILL USE IT IN MY WINTER CASSEROLES WHEN MANY HERBS ARE IN
SHORT SUPPLY.

Ingredients:

6 sprigs parsley, finely chopped

2 sprigs rosemary, finely chopped

4 sage leaves, finely chopped

2 fresh bay leaves

3 garlic cloves, sliced

sea salt and black pepper

1 large chicken

several strips of pršut, bacon or
pancetta

olive oil

- Preheat the oven to 200°C (390°F).
- In a small bowl, combine the herbs and garlic and season lightly with salt and pepper. Scoop out the herb mixture and place inside the chicken.
- Wrap the chicken with the strips of pršut, bacon or pancetta and brush with olive oil and sprinkle lightly with salt and pepper.
- Place the prepared chicken in a roasting pan. Cover and roast for 30 minutes. Remove the lid.
- Reduce the heat to 180°C (350°F) and cook for 20 more minutes or until chicken is tender. The juice should run clear when the chicken is tested with a skewer.

Roast Chicken with Pomegranate and Spinach

THERE ARE TWO VARIETIES OF POMEGRANATE IN RAČIŠĆE — ONE IS SWEETER THAN THE OTHER. TO ME THEY LOOK THE SAME, BUT THE LOCALS SEEM TO BE ABLE TO TELL THEM APART EASILY. BEYOND THE PATH BEHIND OUR HOUSE, ON AN UNUSED PIECE OF LAND IN A SMALL WILDERNESS, WE ARE LUCKY TO HAVE A TREE OF EACH VARIETY.

THIS UNUSUAL COMBINATION PROVIDES A SURPRISING BURST OF FLAVOUR.

Ingredients:

6 skinless chicken thighs

30 grams (about 2 tablespoons) plain flour seasoned with sea salt and black pepper

olive oil

small handful of fresh thyme, finely chopped

sea salt and black pepper

2 garlic cloves, crushed

125 millilitres (½ cup) white wine

seeds from 1 pomegranate

2 handfuls of spinach, washed

- Preheat the oven to 200°C (390°F). Place the chicken and seasoned flour in a large brown paper bag. Shake the bag to coat the chicken pieces thoroughly.
- Place a large frying pan over medium heat and pan-fry the chicken in a small amount of olive oil until lightly browned, turning once.
- Remove the chicken pieces from the pan and place in an ovenproof casserole dish.
- Sprinkle with thyme, salt, pepper and garlic. Pour the wine over the chicken and drizzle with olive oil.
- Roast, covered, for 25 minutes before adding the pomegranate seeds and cooking for 5 more minutes.
- When the chicken is cooked all the way through (the juices should run clear when the chicken is pierced with a skewer), remove from the oven.
- Add the spinach and replace the lid for a few minutes until the spinach wilts. There should be a sauce at the bottom of the pan to pour over the chicken.
- Serve with brown or black rice.

Fisherman's Stew

FISHING HAS BEEN A TRADITIONAL WAY OF LIFE IN THE VILLAGE OF RAČIŠĆE SINCE THE ARRIVAL OF THE FIRST PERMANENT INHABITANTS IN THE 17TH CENTURY. THIS RECIPE FOR *BRODET*, A TRADITIONAL CROATIAN STEW, WAS GIVEN TO ME BY OUR FRIEND PAVO. THE SEAFOOD INGREDIENTS MAY BE VARIED TO SUIT YOUR OWN PREFERENCE.

Ingredients:

3 tablespoons olive oil

1 onion, finely chopped

2 garlic cloves, crushed

2 tablespoons finely chopped parsley

200 grams (7 ounces) tomatoes, diced

250 millilitres (1 cup) dry white wine

1 tablespoon red wine vinegar

juice from ½ lemon

2 bay leaves

200 millilitres (¾ cup) water

sea salt and black pepper, to season

250 grams (9 ounces) mussels

250 grams (9 ounces) squid

250 grams (9 ounces) scampi (prawns), peeled and deveined

250 grams (9 ounces) firm-fleshed white fish

parsley

- Heat the olive oil in a large pan and add the onion, garlic and parsley. Cook gently for 5 minutes.
- Stir in the tomatoes, wine, red wine vinegar, lemon juice, bay leaves and water. Bring to the boil and simmer for 15 minutes. Season with salt and pepper.
- While this mixture is cooking, prepare the mussels by scrubbing them under cold running water. Discard any that do not close when tapped.
- To prepare the squid, pull away the head and tentacles. Discard the innards and the backbone. Peel off the skin, keeping the 2 fins on the sides. Wash in cold water and slice into rings.
- Add the squid, scampi, mussels and fish to the stew and cook slowly until the fish is cooked and the mussels have opened, about 5–10 minutes. Instead of stirring, shake the pot.
- Sprinkle with parsley and serve hot with freshly baked bread.

Vanilla Horseshoe Biscuits

Vanilini kiflići, A TRADITIONAL BISCUIT COATED WITH VANILLA SUGAR, ARE
BAKED THROUGHOUT CROATIA.

Ingredients:

250 grams (about 1 cup) butter

150 grams (about ¾ cup) white sugar

1 egg

250 grams (about 2 cups) plain flour

1 teaspoon baking powder

200 grams (about 1¾ cups) ground
   almonds

100 millilitres (about ½ cup) milk

vanilla sugar

- Preheat the oven to 170°C (340°F) and line a large baking tray with baking paper.
- Beat butter and the first quantity of sugar to a cream. Add the egg and beat well.
- In a small bowl, sift together the flour and baking powder.
- Add the ground almonds alternately with the milk and the flour mixture to the butter and sugar mixture.
- The dough should be firm enough to roll with your hands. If it is too soft (as may be the case if your butter has a high water content) you may need to add a little more flour.
- Shape teaspoon-sized pieces into small snakes by rolling in the palm of your lightly flour-coated hands, before twisting into a horseshoe shape.
- Place on the prepared baking tray and bake for 10–12 minutes until the biscuits are pale golden brown.
- Toss in vanilla sugar while the biscuits are still warm.

Croatian Pepper Biscuits

I ENCOUNTERED *PAPRENJACI* FOR THE FIRST TIME ON CROATIA AIRLINES. THE MOUNTAIN HONEY I PURCHASED ON A RECENT TRIP TO SARAJEVO IS A SUPERB ADDITION ALONG WITH THE GREEN PEPPER TO THESE DISTINCTIVELY FLAVOURED BISCUITS.

Ingredients:

375 grams (about 3 cups) plain flour

125 grams (about ½ cup) cold butter, diced

100 grams (about ½ cup) sugar

100 grams (about ¾ cup) ground walnuts

2 eggs, lightly beaten

1 teaspoon ground cloves

1 tablespoon liquid honey

1 teaspoon ground nutmeg

1 teaspoon ground cinnamon

½ teaspoon green or white pepper

- Preheat the oven to 180°C (350°F). Line a large baking tray with baking paper.
- Sift the flour into a large mixing bowl. Add the butter and rub into the mixture by hand, or pulse in a food processor until the mixture resembles breadcrumbs.
- Add the remainder of the ingredients and mix to a smooth dough. Chill in the fridge for 30 minutes.
- On a lightly floured work surface, roll the dough out to 7–8 mm (¼ inch) thickness. Cut into shapes and transfer to the prepared baking tray.
- Bake for 12–15 minutes until light golden brown. Cool on a wire rack.

Bear's Paws

THIS IS A DELICATE, TRADITIONAL SHORTBREAD KNOWN IN CROATIA AS ŠAPE.
LAST YEAR THE OWNER OF THE SMALL SUPERMARKET IN THE VILLAGE
ALLOWED US TO PICK WHAT WE BELIEVED WAS A WALNUT TREE OWNED
BY HIM. BEFORE WE COULD DO THIS, WE HAD TO DO A LOT OF CLEANING
UP UNDER THE TREE. BECAUSE IT IS A LARGE TREE, WE WERE KEEN TO
GET TO THE LOVELY WALNUTS. WE WERE CONTEMPLATING HARVESTING
THIS YEAR'S CROP WHICH LOOKED PROMISING WHEN WE WERE TOLD WE
COULD NO LONGER PICK IT BECAUSE IT IS OWNED BY A MAN WHO LIVES IN
NEW ZEALAND. WE ASSUMED THE OWNER MUST BE IN THE VILLAGE AND
WANTING THE FRUIT FOR HIMSELF. BUT THE VILLAGE GRAPEVINE TOLD US
OTHERWISE. IT SEEMS THE SUPERMARKET OWNER HAD ONLY ALLOWED US TO
PICK THE TREE BECAUSE HE KNEW WE WOULD CLEAR AWAY ALL THE SCRUB
FROM UNDERNEATH IT AND MAKE THE ACCESS BETTER FOR HIM. THE TREE'S
RIGHTFUL OWNER HAS NOT BEEN BACK TO THE VILLAGE FOR YEARS AND IT IS
UNLIKELY THAT HE WILL RETURN ANYTIME IN THE NEAR FUTURE.

Ingredients:

350 grams (about 2¾ cups) plain flour

200 grams (about ¾ cup) cold butter, diced

200 grams (about ¾ cup) caster sugar

1 egg, lightly beaten

150 grams (about 1¼ cup) ground walnuts

1 teaspoon ground cinnamon

icing (confectioner's) sugar

- Preheat the oven to 170°C (340°F). Grease and lightly flour the special shell-shaped moulds resembling a bear's paw, or use moulds of your choice.
- Place the sifted flour and butter in a food processor and pulse until the mixture resembles breadcrumbs.
- Add the caster sugar, egg, walnuts and cinnamon. Pulse until the dough forms a ball. Then turn out onto a lightly floured board and knead until smooth.
- Press the dough firmly into greased and lightly floured moulds. Place moulds on a baking tray.
- Bake for 12–15 minutes until just beginning to colour.
- Remove from the moulds and dust with icing (confectioner's) sugar.

Walnut Squares

THIS RECIPE REQUIRES SEVERAL EGGS. ON THE FIRST OCCASION WHEN I BAKED THIS CROATIAN LAYERED SPECIALTY CAKE, MY FRIEND PAVO HAD GIVEN ME SEVEN EGGS LAID BY THE HENS HE KEEPS IN A SMALL RUN AT THE BACK OF HIS HOUSE.

'HERE, YOU MUST TAKE THESE. I HAVE TOO MANY. MY HENS LAY THREE AND A HALF EGGS PER WEEK,' HE SAID.

Ingredients:

THE BASE

5 eggs, yolks and whites separated

180 grams (about ¾ cup) caster sugar

150 grams (about 1¼ cup) ground walnuts

6 tablespoons strong black espresso coffee

170 grams (about 1⅓ cups) plain flour, sifted

1 teaspoon baking powder

THE FILLING

3 egg yolks

125 grams (about ½ cup) caster sugar

40 grams (about ⅓ cup) plain flour

350 millilitres (1½ cups) milk

1 vanilla pod

150 grams (⅓ cup) butter, softened

THE TOPPING

150 grams (5 ounces) dark chocolate

70 grams (5 tablespoons) butter

2 tablespoons rakija or rum

- Preheat oven to 180°C (350°F). Line a 20 x 25 centimetre (8 x 10 inch) baking dish with baking paper.
- To make the base, place egg yolks and sugar in a large bowl and whisk until pale. Add the walnuts and coffee.
- Add the sifted flour and baking powder and fold in using a wooden spoon.
- In another bowl, beat the egg whites until stiff peaks form.
- Gently fold the whites into the egg yolk mixture.
- Spread into the baking dish and bake for 30 minutes until firm.
- To make the filling, put egg yolks and half the sugar into a bowl and whisk until pale.
- Add the flour and mix well.
- In a small saucepan over medium heat, combine the milk, remaining sugar and vanilla pod and bring to the boil. Remove from the heat and pour half onto the egg mixture, stirring constantly.
- Pour the egg mixture back into the saucepan. Stir over a low heat until thickened. Remove the vanilla pod. Set aside to cool.
- Place the butter in a large bowl and beat until pale.
- Add the cooled egg yolk mixture to the butter a little at a time. Beat for 3–4 minutes until light and creamy. Pour over the cooked base. Refrigerate until set.
- To make the topping, melt the chocolate and butter in a bowl over a saucepan of simmering water. Add the rakija and mix well. Spread over the top of the cooled cake and refrigerate until set. Cut into squares to serve.

Grape Jelly

PLANTED ONLY LAST YEAR, OUR GRAPEVINES HAVE YET TO BEAR FRUIT.
IN RETURN FOR HELPING OUR FRIEND PAVO PRUNE AND HARVEST HIS
GRAPES, HE GIVES US A LARGE BUCKET OF BLACK EATING GRAPES AND
ALSO ALLOWS US TO PICK THE OVERGROWN VINES ON A PLOT OF LAND HE
NO LONGER CULTIVATES. BUT THE ACCESS IS DIFFICULT. WE MUST HACK
OUR WAY THROUGH SCRUB AND CREEPERS ALONG A PRECARIOUS PATHWAY
LITTERED WITH DEAD APPLIANCES SUCH AS OLD WASHING MACHINES AND
REFRIGERATORS. WHEN AT LAST WE SUCCEED IN HARVESTING THE SMALL
DARK RED GRAPES, THE EFFORT IS WELL WORTH IT. UNTENDED FOR MANY
YEARS AND LACKING CULTIVATION, FERTILIZER AND WATER, THEIR FLAVOUR
IS SURPRISINGLY INTENSE. THEY ARE PERFECT FOR THIS RECIPE.

Ingredients:

2 kilograms (4½ pounds) purple or
   black grapes

white sugar

- Wash and drain the grapes. Place in a jam or large heavy-based saucepan and cook over medium heat until soft. This will take about 15 minutes.

- Place the grapes in a jelly (muslin) bag and leave overnight to drain over a large bowl. Do not squeeze as this may cause the jelly to become cloudy. Discard the grape pulp.

- Measure the collected juice and pour into the jam saucepan.

- Weigh out the equivalent amount of sugar, for example 3 cups of sugar to 3 cups of juice.

- Bring the juice to the boil. Reduce the heat and add the sugar, stirring constantly until the sugar has dissolved.

- Increase the heat and keep the mixture at a rolling boil, stirring from time to time until the jelly becomes thick and sticky. Test a small amount of jelly on a saucer that has been chilled in the freezer. When a skin forms on the sample, the jelly is ready.

- Pour into hot sterilized jars (see note on page 109) and seal.

Pomegranate Jelly

IT'S NOT AN EASY TASK REMOVING THE SKIN AND PITH FROM
POMEGRANATES, BUT THE END RESULT IS WORTH THE EFFORT. THE SHARP
YET SWEET TASTE OF THIS JELLY IS ADDICTIVE.

Ingredients:

10 fully ripe pomegranates

2 tablespoons lemon juice and
a dozen lemon pips (seeds)
secured in a small muslin bag

white sugar

- Break the pomegranates open using a substantial tool such as a meat cleaver, scoop out the flesh and seeds and place in a jam or large heavy-based saucepan. Bring to the boil and cook over medium heat until soft. This will take about 15 minutes.
- Place the pomegranate pulp into a jelly (muslin) bag over a bowl and leave overnight to drain. Do not squeeze the bag or the jelly may become cloudy.
- Measure the collected juice and pour into the jam or large heavy-based saucepan.
- Weigh out the equivalent amount of sugar, for example 1 cup of sugar to 1 cup of juice.
- Add the lemon pips (seeds) and lemon juice to the pomegranate juice and bring to the boil. Reduce the heat and add the sugar, stirring constantly until the sugar has dissolved.
- Increase the heat and keep the mixture at a rolling boil, stirring from time to time until the jelly becomes thick and sticky.
- Test a small amount of jelly on a saucer that has been chilled in the freezer. When a skin forms on the sample, the jelly is ready.
- Remove the muslin bag and ladle the jelly into hot sterilized jars (see note on page 109) and seal.

Rocket (Arugula) Salad with Pomegranate Dressing

THE FLAVOUR IN THIS UNIQUE DRESSING CAN BE ENHANCED BY MAKING IT
AHEAD OF TIME AND LETTING IT STAND BEFORE USE.

Ingredients:

large handful of rocket (arugula)

small handful of fresh basil leaves

20–30 grams (about 1 ounce) blue
  cheese or strong-flavoured hard
  cheese, crumbled

3 teaspoons lemon juice

2 teaspoons liquid honey

4 tablespoons olive oil

2 teaspoons balsamic vinegar

sea salt and black pepper

75 grams (about ½ cup) fresh
  pomegranate seeds

- Arrange the rocket (arugula), basil and cheese in a salad bowl.
- Place the remainder of the ingredients in a small bowl and whisk together until combined.
- Leave the dressing to rest for 30 minutes before pouring over the salad.

Ricotta Almond Tart

ON A RECENT TRIP TO HVAR I CAME ACROSS A WONDERFUL DELICATESSEN
RUN BY A JOVIAL MAN WITH AN ENORMOUS, COMICAL RED NOSE. HE
WAS INTENT ON OFFERING ME SAMPLES OF WHAT SEEMED LIKE HALF OF
HIS STOCK, AND BY THE TIME I LEFT I WAS LADEN WITH ALL SORTS OF
DELECTABLE GOODIES, INCLUDING A JAR OF LOCAL LAVENDER HONEY.
ALTHOUGH I LOVE TO SAVOUR IT ON TOAST FOR BREAKFAST, I SACRIFICED
SOME OF IT TO MAKE THIS RECIPE.

Ingredients:

50 grams (about 1 cup) brioche or fresh
    white breadcrumbs

125 grams (about 1 cup) whole
    almonds

300 grams (about 1¼ cups) ricotta

3 eggs, lightly beaten

zest from half an orange

180 millilitres (¾ cup) liquid honey

- Preheat the oven to 180°C (350°F) and line a 20 centimetre (8 inch) round loose-bottom cake tin with baking paper.
- Spread the breadcrumbs evenly over the bottom of the tin and set aside.
- Put the almonds in a shallow ovenproof dish and bake for 10–15 minutes until lightly browned. Allow to cool. Chop roughly and set aside.
- In a bowl, mix the ricotta and the eggs together. Add the orange zest, honey and chopped almonds. Mix together and pour into the cake tin over the top of breadcrumbs.
- Bake for about 30 minutes or until firm to the touch. Cool before removing from the tin.
- Serve at room temperature.

Pancakes (Palačinke) with Chocolate Sauce and Walnuts

PANCAKES ARE A TRADITIONAL CROATIAN DESSERT. THIS RECIPE WAS
GIVEN TO ME BY NATASHA, A FRIEND FROM THE VILLAGE. SHE SERVED
US *PALAČINKE* FILLED WITH JAM ACCOMPANIED BY A GLASS OF HOMEMADE
PROŠEC (DESSERT WINE) ONE NIGHT WHILE WE WERE WAITING FOR THE
VILLAGE OLIVE PRESS TO OPEN. WHEN I COMPLIMENTED HER ON HOW
SUPERB HER *PALAČINKE* WERE, SHE GAVE ME THE RECIPE. THESE PANCAKES
ARE OFTEN SERVED WITH CHOCOLATE SAUCE SO I HAVE ALSO INCLUDED A
SPECIAL CHOCOLATE SAUCE RECIPE GIVEN TO ME OVER TWENTY YEARS AGO
BY A FRIEND CALLED YVONNE.

Ingredients:

PANCAKES

125 grams (about 1 cup) plain flour

pinch of salt

2 eggs

300 millilitres (1¼ cups) milk

250 millilitres (1 cup) milk

1 vanilla pod

40 grams (about 3 tablespoons) butter

2 tablespoons rakija or rum

1 tablespoon ground walnuts

CHOCOLATE SAUCE

50 grams (about ⅓ cup) cocoa powder

60 millilitres (¼ cup) golden syrup

6 tablespoons water

25 grams (about 2 tablespoons) sugar

pinch of salt

- Preheat the oven to 50°C (120°F) to keep the pancakes warm.

- Sift the flour and salt into a mixing bowl. Make a well in the centre and add the eggs and half the milk. Using a wooden spoon, mix while gradually adding the remaining milk. Beat until the batter is smooth.

- Pour the batter into a jug and refrigerate for 15 minutes.

- Brush a small non-stick frying pan with oil and place over medium heat. Add sufficient batter to thinly coat the base of the pan. Swirl the batter around the pan until it is spread evenly. Cook for 1–2 minutes until batter is set and pale golden in colour. Turn the pancake and cook on the other side. Transfer to a plate and keep warm in the oven.

- Continue to cook the pancakes until all the batter has been used.

- For the chocolate sauce, in a small saucepan mix together the cocoa powder, golden syrup and water. Cook over a low heat until combined.

- Add the sugar, salt, milk and vanilla pod. Bring to the boil and simmer for 10 minutes, stirring occasionally.

- Remove the vanilla pod and add the butter. Beat well. Add rakija or rum.

- Spoon the sauce over the pancakes and fold into quarters. Sprinkle with the ground walnuts.

Lemon and Almond Cake

IT WAS A VERY FUNNY MORNING WHEN I EMBARKED ON CREATING THIS RECIPE USING OLIVE OIL INSTEAD OF BUTTER. I WAS IN THE KITCHEN ASSEMBLING MY INGREDIENTS WHEN I HEARD A COMMOTION OUTSIDE FOLLOWED BY SOMEONE SHOUTING OBSCENITIES. IT WAS IMPOSSIBLE TO IGNORE THE CACOPHONY AND WHEN I HURRIED OUTSIDE, A MAN FROM THE WATERFRONT WHO CLAIMED TO BE THE OWNER OF THE LISBON LEMON TREE WAS LYING ON HIS HEAD UNDERNEATH IT. IT SEEMS HE HAD CLIMBED THE TREE AND STOOD ON A BRANCH THAT WAS NOT STRONG ENOUGH TO HOLD HIS WEIGHT. WHEN THE BRANCH BROKE, MR GREEDY HAD LOST HIS BALANCE AND CRASHED TO THE GROUND. ON HIS WAY DOWN, THE TREE'S SPIKES HAD LACERATED HIM. MY FIRST REACTION WAS TO FEEL SORRY FOR HIM, BUT THEN THE PLASTIC BAG HE HAD BEEN FILLING WITH LEMONS SPLIT OPEN, REVEALING ALMOST THE ENTIRE CROP.

Ingredients:

500 millilitres (2 cups) water

225 grams (about 1 cup) caster sugar

125 millilitres (½ cup) olive oil

juice and zest from 1 large lemon

300 grams (about 2½ cups) self-raising flour

1 teaspoon baking powder

120 grams (about 1 cup) ground almonds

4 eggs, beaten

DRIZZLE ICING

zest and juice from 1 large lemon

icing (confectioner's) sugar

- Preheat the oven to 170°C (340°F). Grease a 20 centimetre (8 inch) round cake tin and line with baking paper.
- Place the water, sugar, olive oil, zest and lemon juice into a large bowl. Mix well.
- Sift together the flour and baking powder.
- Add the flour and almonds to the liquid mixture and mix until smooth.
- Stir in the beaten eggs and mix until combined.
- Spoon the mixture into the prepared cake tin and bake for 1 hour or until a skewer inserted into the middle of the cake comes out clean. Do not overbake.
- Meanwhile, to make the drizzle icing, mix together the lemon juice, zest and enough icing (confectioner's) sugar to make a runny icing.
- When the cake is ready, remove and cool in the tin for 10 minutes, then turn out onto a large flat plate and pour the drizzle icing over it.
- Serve when cool.

Apple and Cinnamon Cake

IT WAS A LATE SUMMER'S DAY WHEN OUR NEIGHBOUR, DARIA, AND HER HUSBAND
INVITED US TO LUNCH ON THE TERRACE AT THE REAR OF THEIR HOUSE,
TOGETHER WITH FRIENDS FROM NEW ZEALAND. EIGHT OF US SAT DOWN TO A
GOURMET SPREAD. THERE WERE VARIOUS VEGETABLE DISHES INCLUDING THE
TRADITIONAL POTATO AND SILVERBEET (CHARD), GRILLED PEPPERS, A SALAD
AND FRESH GREEN BEANS FROM DARIA'S GARDEN. WHEN DARIA'S SON ANDRE
GRILLED THE FISH DARIA HAD CAUGHT EARLY THAT MORNING OVER A FIRE
MADE FROM LAST YEAR'S OLIVE TREE PRUNING, I THOUGHT THE MEAL COULD
NOT GET ANY BETTER. I WAS ALREADY ON THE POINT OF BEING UNABLE TO EAT
OR DRINK ANY MORE WHEN DARIA BROUGHT OUT THIS DELICIOUS CAKE AND
SERVED IT WITH HER ADDICTIVE BLUEBERRY RAKIJA.

Ingredients:

180 grams (about ¾ cup) butter

100 grams (½ cup) sugar

3 eggs

250 grams (about 2 cups) plain flour, sifted

2 teaspoons baking powder

250 millilitres (1 cup) milk

2 tablespoons rakija or rum

zest from 2 lemons

5 medium apples, peeled and thinly sliced

¾ cup grated apple

4 teaspoons vanilla sugar

2 teaspoons cinnamon

- Preheat the oven to 170°C (340°F). Line a deep, medium-sized baking dish with baking paper.
- Beat the butter and sugar to a cream. In a separate bowl, beat the eggs until thick. Add to the butter mixture and beat until smooth.
- Add the sifted flour and baking powder alternately with the milk. Add the rakija and lemon zest.
- Spread half the mixture into the baking dish. Bake for 20 minutes.
- Remove from the oven and cover with apple slices followed by the remainder of the cake mixture.
- Bake for 25–30 more minutes until golden brown.
- Mix together the grated apple, vanilla sugar and cinnamon and spread this over the top of the cake while it is still hot.

Adriatic Almond Biscuits

NOT ONLY ARE THESE BISCUITS IRRESISTIBLE, THEY ARE ALSO
SUITABLE FOR ANYONE WHO IS GLUTEN INTOLERANT.

Ingredients:

300 grams (about 2½ cups) ground almonds

300 grams (about 2½ cups) icing (confectioner's) sugar, plus extra for rolling

3 egg whites

2 teaspoons liquid honey

flaked almonds, fig or cherry jam

- In a large bowl, mix together the ground almonds and icing (confectioner's) sugar. Add the egg whites and honey and mix until a smooth dough is formed.
- Cover the bowl and rest the dough in the refrigerator for 30 minutes.
- Preheat the oven to 150°C (300°F). Line a baking tray with baking paper.
- Divide the dough into 4 equal pieces. Dust your work surface with icing (confectioner's) sugar. Roll each piece of dough into a sausage shape. Slice each sausage into 8 equal pieces. Shape each piece into rounds and place on the prepared tray. Using your finger or thumb, press an indent into each round.
- Fill the indents with a small quantity of jam or flaked almonds.
- Once the biscuits are filled, place the baking tray in the freezer for 10 minutes.
- Place in the preheated oven and bake for 15 minutes or until the biscuits are pale golden brown. Cool before removing from the tray.
- Store in an airtight container.

Winter

The coldest time of the year is from December until February. Often it's extremely wet, but there are days when it can be surprisingly dry and sunny too. However, it is mostly mild by continental European winter standards, with minimal frosts. It seldom snows on the coast, although it has been known to fall. For me, the gourmet delight in early winter is mushrooms. There are about 30 different varieties that grow here in cycles. They are commonly found hidden in the leaf mulch underneath olive trees. This year we have been privileged to learn about several of the special spots around the village where mushrooms are usually found. In Pavo's family these places are a heavily guarded secret handed down from father to son, through the generations. On the first occasion we went mushrooming with Pavo, it was a Sunday morning. He said this was one of the best times to forage because many of the villagers were at church and they would not see where he went or how many mushrooms he found.

There are many ways to enjoy eating mushrooms. They are fantastic grilled, in casseroles, risotto or in soup.

Winter is the time to slow down, taste and enjoy the fruits of the land harvested during the remainder of the year. There is nothing finer than eating preserved, seasonal delights with a glass of red wine in front of a blazing open fire.

Mushroom Soup

MY FIRST POT OF MUSHROOM SOUP WAS MADE HERE USING ONLY ONE
CHAMPIGNON. THIS GIANT OF ALL MUSHROOMS WAS THE SIZE OF A
DINNER PLATE.

THIS RECIPE WAS GIVEN TO ME BY ANITA, THE AFRICAN CHEF TO THE
NEW ZEALAND AMBASSADOR IN HARARE DURING 1994.

Ingredients:

1 tablespoon butter

1 small onion, finely sliced

250 grams (about 2 cups) mushrooms,
  sliced

1 tablespoon flour

500 millilitres (2 cups) chicken or
  vegetable stock

1 tablespoon finely chopped fresh
  thyme

sea salt and black pepper

- Heat the butter and fry the onion until soft and transparent. Add the mushrooms and sauté for about 5 minutes.
- Stir in the flour and cook for 2 minutes. Allow to cool slightly.
- Add the stock gradually.
- Cover and simmer gently for 20 minutes.
- Add the thyme and season to taste.

Leek and Potato Soup

THE RICH RED VOLCANIC SOIL IN OUR OLIVE GROVE AT VRVALA SEEMED
LIKE A GOOD PLACE TO PLANT A CROP OF POTATOES. UNFORTUNATELY,
THE SOIL PROVED DIFFICULT TO TILL AS IT WAS MANY YEARS SINCE IT HAD
BEEN TURNED OVER. WE WERE CONSIDERING STOPPING WORK FOR THE DAY
WHEN A CAR PULLED UP ADJACENT TO WHERE WE HAD BEEN WORKING. A
KIND MAN FROM THE VILLAGE HAD BROUGHT ALONG HIS ROTARY HOE. YOU
CAN IMAGINE OUR DELIGHT WHEN HE MADE AN EASY JOB OF TILLING OUR
POTATO PLOT.

Ingredients:

3–4 large leeks, washed, sliced lengthways first, then finely crossways (discard the coarse green tops)

10–12 medium potatoes, peeled or unpeeled, roughly chopped

3 garlic cloves, crushed

1 stick celery, finely sliced

2 large onions, sliced

1 tablespoon olive oil

1 tablespoon butter

750 millilitres (3 cups) vegetable stock

125 millilitres (½ cup) dry white wine (optional)

3 bay leaves

sea salt and black pepper

sour cream, chopped parsley

- Over medium heat, sauté the leeks, potatoes, garlic, celery and onions in olive oil and butter in a large covered saucepan for 10–15 minutes until the onion becomes transparent.
- Add the vegetable stock, wine and bay leaves. Bring to the boil and simmer covered for 1 hour until the vegetables are soft. Cool slightly.
- Remove the bay leaves and purée the soup in a food processor.
- Season to taste with salt and pepper. If necessary, thin with extra vegetable stock or water.
- Serve hot with sour cream, chopped parsley and freshly baked bread or toast.

Silverbeet (Chard) and Potatoes

A TRADITIONAL CROATIAN VEGETABLE DISH. MY GRANDMOTHER COOKED THIS DISH OFTEN USING THE ENDLESS SUPPLY OF SILVERBEET (CHARD) FROM HER VEGETABLE GARDEN.

Ingredients:

6 medium potatoes, peeled or unpeeled, roughly chopped

4 large stalks silverbeet (chard), washed and roughly chopped

3 tablespoons olive oil

2 garlic cloves, crushed

juice from 1 lemon

sea salt and black pepper

- In a large heavy-based saucepan, boil the potatoes in salted water for 15–20 minutes until they are tender. During the last 5 minutes of the potatoes cooking, add silverbeet (chard).
- Drain the vegetables and tip into a large serving bowl or dish. Add the olive oil, garlic, lemon juice, salt and pepper.
- Toss to combine or mash the vegetables together. Serve hot.

Roast Potatoes with Rosemary and Lemon

It is just as well our lemon tree produces an overabundance of lemons because the Lisbon tree is no longer. The man who fell out of it became so angry on this particular day that he forbade us to continue watering it. Now the locals wander up Flower Street and shake their heads in despair at the withered sad skeleton. Under their breaths they mutter about the foolish behaviour of the greedy man from the waterfront.

Ingredients:

1½ kilograms (3⅓ pounds) potatoes, peeled or unpeeled

60 millilitres (¼ cup) water

6 sprigs rosemary, roughly chopped

sea salt and black pepper

olive oil

juice from 2 lemons

- Preheat the oven to 190°C (375°F). Cut the potatoes into long fingers and place in a large roasting dish lined with baking paper.
- Pour the water over the potatoes and sprinkle with the rosemary, salt and pepper. Drizzle with the olive oil.
- Roast for about 45 minutes, turning the potatoes once or twice. Pour the lemon juice over them and continue to roast for 15 more minutes until golden brown. Cooking time may vary depending on the variety of potatoes. Serve hot.

Gnocchi with Meat Sauce

THIS TRADITIONAL PASTA DISH CAN BE FOUND IN MANY AREAS OF CROATIA. IT IS MORE OFTEN FOUND ON THE COAST WHERE THE ITALIAN INFLUENCE IS STRONG. I CREATED THIS RECIPE AFTER CONSULTATION WITH MIKE, A CHEF FROM CUBA STREET, WELLINGTON, A FAMOUS FOODIE AREA IN NEW ZEALAND'S CAPITAL CITY.

Ingredients:

GNOCCHI

500 grams (about 1 pound) potatoes, peeled

1 egg, lightly beaten

125 grams (about 1 cup) plain flour

50 grams (about ½ cup) parmesan cheese, grated

good pinch of nutmeg

sea salt and black pepper

MEAT SAUCE

2 tablespoons olive oil

1 medium onion, sliced

2 garlic cloves, crushed

500 grams (about 1 pound) lean minced meat (I use a mixture of veal, beef and lamb for a richer flavour)

500 millilitres (2 cups) beef stock

handful of fresh basil

1 tablespoon fresh oregano, chopped

2 medium tomatoes, diced

1 capsicum (bell pepper), finely sliced

2 tablespoons tomato paste

1 teaspoon paprika

sea salt and black pepper

grated parmesan cheese

- In a large saucepan over high heat, boil the potatoes in salted water for 15 minutes or until tender. Drain and cool slightly. Mash until smooth.
- Place the potatoes and the remaining ingredients into a large bowl and mix until smooth. Season with the salt and pepper. The dough should be soft.
- Fill another large saucepan with salted water, place over high heat and bring to the boil.
- On a lightly floured work surface roll portions of the dough into 1½ centimetre (⅔ inch) diameter sausage shapes. Cut into 2½ centimetre (1 inch) long pieces.
- Cook the gnocchi in batches in the boiling water. Remove from the water, using a slotted spoon, when they float to the surface. Place the cooked gnocchi into a bowl of iced water. Repeat with the remaining dough.
- For the meat sauce, sauté the onion and garlic in the olive oil in a large non-stick frying pan until the onion becomes transparent.
- Add the minced meat and stir continuously until the meat has browned. Then cook for 2 more minutes.
- Add the stock, basil, oregano, tomatoes, capsicum (bell pepper), tomato paste and paprika. Bring to the boil.
- Reduce the heat and simmer for 45 minutes until the mixture has reduced and thickened. Season to taste.
- Place the gnocchi carefully into the meat sauce and heat gently for 5 minutes.
- Sprinkle with the parmesan cheese and serve hot.

Oven Baked Octopus

I DISCOVERED THIS SENSATIONAL DISH DURING A LONG LUNCH WITH FRIENDS AT A *KONOBA* (TRADITIONAL CROATIAN RESTAURANT) IN THE NEARBY VILLAGE OF PUPNAT. IT HAD BEEN COOKED OVER THE EMBERS OF AN OPEN FIRE UNDERNEATH A *PEKA*, THE TRADITIONAL CROATIAN FORM OF A TAGINE. THE FLAVOUR OF THE DISH WAS OUTSTANDING AND THE OCTOPUS WAS EXCEPTIONALLY TENDER. THIS CASSEROLE IS ALMOST AS EXCEPTIONAL WHEN COOKED IN A CONVENTIONAL OVEN.

Ingredients:

1 kilogram octopus (2¼ pounds), pre-frozen and thawed

400 grams (about 1 pound) potatoes, peeled or unpeeled and sliced

4 tablespoons olive oil

200 grams (about 1 cup) tomatoes, chopped

1 medium onion, sliced

3 garlic cloves, crushed

1 red capsicum (bell pepper), deseeded and sliced

4 sprigs rosemary

sea salt and black pepper

125 millilitres (½ cup) dry white wine

- Preheat the oven to 200°C (390°F).
- Cut the octopus into thumb-sized pieces.
- Cover the bottom of a large ovenproof casserole dish with the potatoes. Add 2 tablespoons of the olive oil.
- Add the octopus, tomatoes, onion, garlic, red capsicum (bell pepper) and rosemary, and season with salt and pepper.
- Pour over remaining olive oil and wine.
- Bake covered for 45–60 minutes until the octopus is tender when tested with a fork. Serve hot.

Croatian Cod Stew

BAKALAR IS TRADITIONALLY EATEN ON CHRISTMAS EVE. I REMEMBER THE
FIRST TIME I ATE THIS STEW IN CROATIA. WHEN WE WERE INVITED TO
PAVO'S HOUSE ON CHRISTMAS EVE I KNEW WE WOULD BE EATING *BAKALAR*.
WALKING DOWN THE COBBLED ALLEYWAY TOWARDS HIS HOUSE MY MOUTH
BEGAN TO WATER AS THE AROMA OF IT COOKING DRIFTED TOWARDS ME.
BUT ALAS, HIS WIFE HAD NOT TAKEN ENOUGH CARE OVER THE PREPARATION
OF THE STEW. WHAT SHOULD HAVE BEEN A TASTY MEAL TURNED OUT TO BE
A MOUTHFUL OF OILY, SALTY BONES. AFTER TASTING NO MORE THAN THE
FIRST MOUTHFUL, PAVO ERUPTED AND SHOUTED, 'MY WIFE, SHE IS LAZY!'

Ingredients:

500 grams (about 1 pound) dried
   salted cod

1 large onion, finely sliced

4 garlic cloves, crushed

2 tablespoons parsley, finely
   chopped

olive oil

1 kilogram (2¼ pounds) potatoes,
   diced

sea salt and black pepper

- Wash the salted cod and soak overnight in cold water.
- Wash again, then place in a large saucepan and cover with fresh water. Cook slowly, covered over a low heat until it is tender. This will take about 4 hours.
- Remove the cod, drain and reserve liquid.
- Carefully remove the bones and discard them.
- Sauté the onion, garlic and parsley in olive oil. Add the potatoes and stir until they are coated with oil.
- Add the reserved liquid and cook until the potatoes are tender.
- Return cod to the pot.
- Simmer gently for 20 minutes. Season with salt and pepper and serve with freshly baked, crusty bread.

Slavonian Pork Casserole

PORK FROM CORN-FED PIGS IN SLAVONIA IN THE NORTH-EAST IS A POPULAR
MEAT IN CROATIA. IT IS ALWAYS TENDER AND IS GUARANTEED TO PROVIDE A
FLAVOURSOME INGREDIENT IN ANY DISH.

Ingredients:

50 millilitres (about 3 tablespoons)
   olive oil

2 onions, finely sliced

2 garlic cloves, sliced

150 grams (5 ounces) pršut or pancetta,
   finely sliced

500 grams (about 1 pound) pork, any
   cut, cubed

200 grams (7 ounces) mushrooms,
   sliced

200 grams (7 ounces) kulen or spicy
   salami, sliced

1 teaspoon paprika

4 tablespoons tomato purée or 3 fresh
   tomatoes, finely diced

400 grams (14 ounces) potatoes, diced

½ small cabbage, finely sliced

3 tablespoons parsley, chopped plus
   extra to serve

400 millilitres (1⅔ cup) dry white wine

400 millilitres (1⅔ cup) beef or chicken
   stock

sea salt and black pepper

- Preheat the oven to 170°C (340°F).
- Heat the oil in a large cast-iron casserole dish and fry the onions and garlic until soft. Add the pršut or pancetta and continue to fry for 4 more minutes.
- Add the pork and mushrooms and fry until lightly browned.
- Stir in the remaining ingredients and cover with the stock.
- Place in the oven and bake, covered, for 2–2½ hours until the meat is tender.
- Serve hot, sprinkled with parsley, and accompanied by freshly baked bread.

Dalmatian Shepherd's Lamb with Potatoes and Broad Beans

ON THE COAST, SHEEP IN CROATIA DRINK SALT WATER WHILE IN THE INTERIOR THEY GRAZE ON WILD HERBS. LAMB IN CROATIA HAS A STRONG CHARACTERISTIC FLAVOUR.

Ingredients:

4 tablespoons olive oil

1 onion, finely sliced

3 garlic cloves, finely sliced

800 grams (1¾ pounds) lamb off the bone, loin or leg, diced

3–4 tomatoes, skinned and diced

1 small stalk celery, finely diced

500 grams (about 1 pound) new potatoes

2 bay leaves

2 sprigs rosemary

sea salt and black pepper

125 millilitres (½ cup) red wine

500 millilitres (2 cups) beef stock

250 grams (about 1 cup) fresh broad beans

chopped parsley

- Preheat the oven to 170°C (340°F).
- Over medium heat, fry the onion in olive oil in a heavy-based saucepan until transparent.
- Add the garlic and lamb. Fry until the meat is light brown.
- Transfer to an ovenproof casserole dish. Add the tomatoes, celery, potatoes, bay leaves, rosemary, salt and pepper to taste, and red wine.
- Cover with half the stock and bake covered for 2–2½ hours until the meat is tender.
- Add the broad beans and extra stock and cook for an additional 10–15 minutes.
- Remove from the oven and sprinkle with chopped parsley.
- Serve with freshly baked bread and a glass of full-bodied red wine such as Mali Plavac or Zinfandel.

Bowknots

KNOWN IN CROATIA AS *KROŠTULE*, THESE LIGHT, FESTIVE TEMPTATIONS
ARE ANOTHER TRADITIONAL CROATIAN DELIGHT. DURING MY
CHILDHOOD, MY GRANDMOTHER ALWAYS SERVED HER MOUNTAIN OF
KROŠTULE ON A BEAUTIFUL OVAL DISH PATTERNED WITH BIG PINK ROSES
AND EDGED WITH GOLD.

Ingredients:

500 grams (about 4 cups) plain flour

2 teaspoons baking powder

good pinch of salt

2 eggs

50 grams (about ¼ cup) sugar

50 grams (about 3½ tablespoons)
    butter, melted

2 tablespoons (or more, to taste) rakija
    or rum

zest from 1 orange and 1 lemon

100 millilitres (about ½ cup) milk

sunflower oil

icing (confectioner's) sugar to dust

- Sift the flour, baking powder and salt into a bowl.
- In another bowl, beat the eggs and sugar until light and frothy.
- Add the butter, rakija, orange and lemon zest.
- Add the egg mixture to the flour mixture and stir with a wooden spoon.
- Mix in sufficient milk to make a soft dough.
- On a lightly floured work surface, knead the dough for 5 minutes. Place in a lightly floured bowl and cover with a baking cloth or clean tea towel. Leave to rest for 30 minutes in a warm place.
- Turn the dough out and break it into 6 pieces. Roll each piece into a thin sheet and cut into 1½ centimetre (⅔ inch) wide strips about 10 centimetres (4 inches) long. Tie each strip into a knot or bow.
- In a heavy-based saucepan add sufficient oil to cover the bowknots and allow them to float. Bring to high heat. Deep fry the bowknots in hot oil, a few at a time, until golden brown. Lift out with a slotted spoon and drain on kitchen paper.
- Dust with icing (confectioner's) sugar while hot.

Walnut and Coffee Slice

DURING THE 1960S AND 1970S, GREEN COFFEE BEANS WERE SMUGGLED ILLEGALLY FROM ITALY INTO YUGOSLAVIA AND SOLD ON THE BLACK MARKET. IN MORE RECENT TIMES A DIFFERENT FORM OF SMUGGLING TAKES PLACE. TRUCKS CARRYING SACKS OF GREEN BEANS FROM EUROPE STOP OVERNIGHT, BESIDE THE RIVER, IN THE FOG. GREEN COFFEE BEANS ARE HYGROSCOPIC WHICH MEANS THEY HAVE THE ABILITY TO ABSORB MOISTURE OF UP TO 3 PER CENT. BEFORE CONTINUING HIS JOURNEY, THE DRIVER REMOVES JUST ENOUGH BEANS TO KEEP THE WEIGHT THE SAME AS IT WAS BEFORE HE ENTERED THE FOG AREA. AS IN EARLIER TIMES, THE CUNNING INDIVIDUAL THEN SELLS THE BEANS ON THE BLACK MARKET.

Ingredients:

BASE

4 eggs, yolks and whites separated

180 grams (about 1 cup) brown sugar

200 grams (about 1½ cups) medium ground walnuts

TOPPING

200 grams (about ¾ cup) butter

150 grams (about ¾ cup) brown sugar

1 egg yolk

4 tablespoons cold strong black espresso coffee

100 grams (about ¾ cup) medium ground walnuts

- Preheat oven to 150°C (300°F). Line a 20 x 25 centimetre (8 x 10 inch) baking dish with baking paper.
- Beat the egg yolks and brown sugar until thick and glossy.
- In a separate bowl, beat the egg whites until stiff.
- Add the walnuts to the yolk mixture and combine. Gently fold in the egg whites.
- Place the baking dish in the oven and bake for 25–30 minutes until pale golden brown.
- Remove from oven and allow to cool.
- To make the topping, beat the butter and sugar to a cream.
- Add the egg yolk and beat again to combine.
- Mix in the espresso coffee.
- Spread this over the cooled base and sprinkle with the walnuts. Gently press the walnuts into the topping with your hand to make sure it is evenly coated.
- Place in the refrigerator to set.
- Cut into slices to serve.

Limoncello

EVERY YEAR WE DISTIL RAKIJA USING THE GRAPE SKINS LEFT OVER FROM OUR WINE MAKING. THE SKINS ARE LEFT TO FERMENT IN SUGAR FOR SEVERAL WEEKS BEFORE WE TAKE THEM, TOGETHER WITH A SUPPLY OF FIREWOOD, TO THE STILL ON THE OUTSKIRTS OF THE VILLAGE. RADE, WHO LEARNT THIS TRADE FROM HIS FATHER, OPERATES THE CHARRED BLACK STILL. A LENGTHY PROCEDURE, IT TAKES SEVERAL HOURS BEFORE THE FIRST DROPS OF ALCOHOL EMERGE. BY THE TIME THE PROCESS IS FINISHED, WE ARE USUALLY REWARDED WITH AT LEAST FIVE LITRES OF RAKIJA.

Ingredients:

12 lemons

2 x 750 millilitres (2 x 25 fluid ounces) bottles of vodka or rakija

500 millilitres (2 cups) water

380 grams (about 2 cups) sugar

- Remove the rind from the lemons, taking care to scrape off any pith. Slice the rind into small pieces.

- Place the rind in a large jar with a screwtop lid and add one bottle of vodka. Store the mixture in a dark place for 2 weeks.

- Combine the water and sugar in a saucepan and bring to the boil over medium heat, stirring constantly until the sugar has dissolved. Cool to room temperature. If the sugar syrup is still warm, the limoncello will be cloudy.

- Strain the vodka from the peel using a fine sieve and mix it with the remaining bottle of vodka and the sugar syrup.

- Bottle and seal tightly.

- Store in a dark place for at least 10 days before drinking.

- To drink straight, limoncello can be stored in the freezer.

Sugared Almonds

My neighbour, Daria, shared this recipe with me. Seated at her kitchen table covered with a red and green plastic tablecloth, I wrote down the recipe while she demonstrated the method. Always hospitable, she insisted I must partake of a glass of her homemade blueberry rakija. One glass led to another and by the time the almonds were sugared, I had drunk several. I couldn't resist the temptation. At the end of the evening, when I stumbled home, I had remembered to bring the recipe with me.

Ingredients:

200 grams (about 1¾ cups) whole raw almonds

200 grams (about 1 cup) white sugar

200 millilitres (about ¾ cup) water

- Preheat the oven to 170°C (340°F). Line a baking tray with baking paper.
- Place the almonds on the prepared tray and roast for 10–15 minutes until the almonds are just beginning to turn brown.
- Place the sugar and water into a heavy-based saucepan and boil over high heat until the mixture is reduced by about half, about 20 minutes. The syrup should be thick but clear.
- Add the almonds. When crystals begin to appear around the edges of the saucepan, reduce the heat to low and stir constantly until the almonds are coated with the white sugar crystals.
- Tip onto another tray lined with baking paper. Cool and break apart any almonds that may have stuck together.
- Store in an airtight jar.

Double Chocolate Fig Truffles

A SPECIAL TREAT FOR CHRISTMAS AND ALSO ONE OF MY BROTHER
COLIN'S FAVOURITE INDULGENCES.

Ingredients:

150 grams (5 ounces) dried figs

60 millilitres (¼ cup) rakija or brandy

90 grams (about 6 tablespoons) butter, melted

200 grams (about 2 cups) cake crumbs

60 grams (about ⅓ cup) icing (confectioner's) sugar

1 teaspoon vanilla

30 grams (about ¼ cup) cocoa powder

1 tablespoon fig jam

20 grams (about ¼ cup) desiccated coconut, plus extra

- Soak the figs in rakija or brandy for a minimum of 3 hours or overnight.
- Tip the soaked figs into a food processor and chop finely.
- In a medium-sized bowl, combine the melted butter with remaining ingredients.
- Add the fig mixture and mix well.
- Shape the mixture into balls by hand and roll in the extra coconut.
- Refrigerate to set.

Doughnuts Filled with Jam

ONE OF MY FAVOURITE CROATIAN INDULGENCES, *KRAFNE*, CAN BE FOUND IN BAKERIES ALL OVER THE COUNTRY. OUR REGULAR TRIPS TO SPLIT ALWAYS INCLUDE A VISIT TO THE BAKERY AT THE TOP END OF KRALJA ZVONIMIRA WHERE A 'HOLE IN THE WALL' BAKERY SELLS THE ABSOLUTE BEST *KRAFNE*.

Ingredients:

250 grams (about 2 cups) plain flour

8 grams (about 1 tablespoon) fresh yeast, crumbled

25 grams (about 2 tablespoons) sugar

30 grams (about 2 tablespoons) butter, melted

good pinch of salt

3 egg yolks

2 tablespoons rakija or rum

125 millilitres (½ cup) milk

sunflower oil for deep frying

pomegranate jelly (see recipe on page 79)

icing (confectioner's) sugar

- Sift the flour into a large bowl. Rub in the yeast using your fingertips. Add sugar, melted butter, salt and egg yolks. Mix in the rakija and milk using a knife.

- Transfer to a stand mixer and continue to mix using the dough hook on an electric mixer, or beat by hand with a wooden spoon, until dough becomes smooth and shiny.

- Place the dough in a lightly floured bowl, cover with a baking cloth or clean tea towel and leave in a warm place to rise for 1¼–1½ hours.

- Remove the dough from the bowl and knead for 5 minutes on a lightly floured surface.

- Roll the dough into a large circle that is 2 centimetre (¾ inch) thick. Cut into 6 centimetre (2¼ inch) circles using a glass or round cookie cutter. Re-knead the remaining dough and repeat until all the dough has been used. Place the circles on a baking tray lined with baking paper and leave to rise in a warm in a warm place (about 30°C, or 85°F) for 20 minutes.

- In a medium-sized heavy-based saucepan, heat ½ litre (2 cups) of oil over low to medium heat. The oil should be hot enough to fry, but not so hot it is smoking.

- Fry the *krafne* one at a time until pale golden brown, turning once after 1–2 minutes. There should be a pale ring around the centre of each krafne.

- Remove from the oil with a slotted spoon and place on kitchen paper to drain.

- Make a small hole into the centre of each *krafne*, using a cooking syringe, and pipe in the pomegranate jelly.

- Sprinkle with icing (confectioner's) sugar while warm.

Christmas Fruit Cake

THIS IS A RECIPE FOR MY VERY OWN CHRISTMAS CAKE CREATED USING NUTS AND DRIED FRUIT FROM OUR SUMMER HARVEST. EVERY NOVEMBER I LOOK FORWARD TO BAKING THIS CHRISTMAS CAKE BECAUSE IT IS SIMPLY THE BEST.

Ingredients:

950 grams dried fruit (I use a mixture of dried raisins, dried figs and prunes in the following approximate quantities: 500 grams (about 3 cups) raisins, 250 grams (about 1½ cups) dried figs, 200 grams (about 1¼ cup) prunes; currants, sultanas, dried apricots, glace cherries and mixed peel can be substituted for up to 100 grams (about ⅔ cup) of the above)

rind from 2 lemons, finely chopped

4 tablespoons rakija, whisky or brandy

8 eggs, at room temperature

350 grams (about 1½ cups) butter

350 grams (about 1⅔ cups) brown sugar

220 grams (about 1⅔ cups) white flour, sifted

3 teaspoons mixed spices (cinnamon, cloves, allspice and nutmeg)

150 grams (about 1¼ cups) almonds, roughly chopped

150 grams (about 1¼ cups) walnuts, roughly chopped

2 tablespoons golden syrup

- Four days before baking the cake, chop the dried figs and prunes into small pieces.
- In a large ceramic or glass bowl, mix all the dried fruit and the lemon rind together. Add the alcohol and stir to combine well.
- Cover and leave for a minimum of 4 days, stirring occasionally. Add a little more alcohol during the process if desired. The dried fruit must be plumped up and well hydrated.
- Preheat the oven to 140°C (280°F). Double line the bottom and sides of a round 20 centimetre (8 inch) cake tin with 2 layers of baking paper stuck together. Extend the paper 5 centimetres (2 inches) above the sides of the tin.
- In a medium-sized bowl, beat the eggs until thick and frothy. Set aside.
- In a large mixing bowl cream the butter and sugar. Add the eggs very slowly, beating well after each addition. Do not add too much at a time or the mixture will curdle.
- Combine the flour with the spices and the chopped nuts.
- Add the golden syrup. Then fold in the flour, spice and nut mixture. Add the mixed fruit and stir well.
- Spoon the mixture into the cake tin and smooth the top flat using a spatula. The cake should rise a small amount only and the surface should remain flat. Carefully drop the cake

tin from a height of 12 centimetres (or 5 inches) onto the floor to make sure there are no air bubbles inside.

- Bake for 2½–3 hours before testing with a skewer (the cooking time may vary with individual ovens). The skewer should come out clean and the cake should have shrunk away from the sides of the tin. If the skewer is not clean, continue baking for 10 more minutes before retesting.

- Remove from the oven when cooked and cool completely in tin. The following day, remove the baking paper and make skewer holes through to the bottom of the cake. Pour over 2 tablespoons of alcohol.

- Repeat this process every 5 days for several weeks. Keep the cake wrapped in foil. Store in an airtight container.

Glossary and cooking notes

General Ingredients

PEPPERCORNS
Black

The more common, hottest and most pungent of all the varieties, this ancient spice was once traded as currency. Today, it remains the most widely traded spice in the world. Black peppercorns are green ones cooked in hot water and sun-dried.

Green

These are unripe black peppercorns often preserved in vinegar or brine and served pickled. In dried form they are available from delicatessens or supermarkets. Use quickly because they do not keep well. They have a milder, fresher flavour.

White

This is the seed of the black peppercorn with the skin removed. White peppercorns are less strong and are earthier in flavour than black peppercorns.

Breadmaking Hints

Salt

Salt is very important in the bread-making process. It assists fermentation, improves the colour and flavour of the loaf, helps develop the crust and ensures the loaf retains its freshness for longer.

Water

Most of my bread and dough recipes do not specify the quantity of tepid water required to form the dough. This is because amounts of water may vary depending on the type of flour. Add water a little at a time to avoid making your dough too wet. Use a knife to mix in the tepid water.

Yeast

I prefer to use fresh yeast which can be bought at delicatessens or supermarkets. Dried yeast is often too strong in flavour and activation. If you choose to use dried yeast, as a general rule, the ratio is one teaspoon of yeast to one cup of flour. Add the dried yeast to the flour as if it is fresh crumbled yeast. There is no need to dissolve it in warm water or add sugar.

Kneading the dough

Turn the sticky dough onto a lightly floured work surface. Slap the dough down and stretch it quite aggressively with lightly floured hands. Continue slapping and stretching to ensure air is trapped inside the dough. As you work, and the dough becomes smoother, you should be able to discontinue using flour. At the end of 8–10 minutes you should have a smooth, elastic dough, ready to shape into a ball.

Forming the dough into a ball

Place dough onto a lightly floured work surface and flatten slightly. Fold all 4 sides of the dough into the centre and press down. Rotating the dough ball, continue to fold in the edges and flatten the ball slightly at the same time. At the end of the kneading process, turn the dough ball over, stretch, tuck and press the edges underneath to form a spine or seam.

Developing a crust on your loaf

To ensure your bread has a firm, unbroken crust and a healthy colour, it can be helpful to add some steam into the oven. The easiest way to mist the oven is by using a clean spray bottle filled with water. Spray 15 squirts before putting your loaf into the hot oven, and another 5 once it is in the oven. Make sure you are close to the oven, only a few centimetres away. Close the door as quickly as practicable to keep the steam contained.

Sterilization of jars

Wash jars and lids well in hot soapy water. Place clean wet jars and lids separately in the oven. Heat to 100℃ (210°F). Turn off after 15 minutes.

Index

About the artist

Colin Unkovich has been airbrush painting since the late 1970s, and working as a full-time artist since 2006. Based in Northland, New Zealand, he is one of New Zealand's most skilled airbrush artists. His finely detailed contemporary artworks often feature very smooth transitions of colour which give each of his works a unique feel or sense of mood. He is self-taught and has developed many special techniques allowing him to highlight the interplay of light and shadow that can give a transient form or a fleeting glimpse, an almost sculptural quality. Colin draws his inspiration from the natural forms of New Zealand, particularly the coast and from the effect that its unusual quality of light possesses.

Colin aims to create paintings that bring pleasure to the eye and give a true sense of the subject while sometimes leaving enough latitude for individual interpretation, to allow the brain to engage and finish the story.

When Colin visited Croatia in 2008 he was inevitably attracted to the natural unspoilt beauty of the island of Korčula. It became a natural progression for Colin to create the artwork for his sister Barbara's books.

Colin's paintings hang in private collections in New Zealand, the United Kingdom, United States of America and Europe. His website is www.colinunkovich.com.